God cares about the BIG things, the small things, and All things in your life.

365 encouraging reflections to inspire you month by month

Inspired by Faith

God cares about the BIG things, the small things,
and ALL things in your life.

ISBN 978-0-9914172-7-8

Published by Product Concept Mfg., Inc.
2175 N. Academy Circle #200, Colorado Springs, CO 80909

©2014 Product Concept Mfg., Inc. All rights reserved

Written and Compiled by Patricia Mitchell, Vicki J. Kuyper
in association with Product Concept, Inc.

God
cares about
the BIG things,
the small things,
and All things
in your life.

Do everything
you can ...
then leave
the rest
to God.

January

He brought me out into a spacious place...
because he delighted in me.
Psalm 18:19 NIV

A brand new year has opened! How do you feel about it? You have a choice, you know. You can choose to take your plans and expectations seriously, but not yourself...to answer carelessness with kindness, confusion with peace, and misunderstanding with wisdom. You can choose to be an influence, an encourager, a forgiver, and an inspiration to others. A tall order? No and no.

It's not tall, because, no matter where today finds you, these things are within your reach. They're as close as your loved ones, your friends, your neighbors, and your coworkers. It's not an order, either, but a privilege God gives you every day to live purposefully and discover happiness...to change lives for the better and fulfill your own...make a difference and enjoy doing it...to give of yourself and receive much, much more in return.

This year, choose to do everything that God has put within reach of your hands and your heart, and then leave the rest to Him. Choose to look ahead with faith, confidence, joy, and a smile!

JANUARY

1

*Write it on your heart that every day
is the best day in the year.*
Ralph Waldo Emerson

It all begins with attitude—a good one, that is! A happy outlook and willingness to do your part despite the circumstances is what moves a bad day to a good day, and a good day to your best day. Plan today with a smile, and you might be surprised at how much of the day smiles back at you—it really works!

2

*Remember, even God took six days
to create the world!*

You may not be able to accomplish great things today, or reach a goal that lies ahead of you, but you can to this: you can start. You can take a step in the right direction by getting organized, making contact with others who can help, or gathering practical, relevant information. Even a small step forward puts you closer to your objective than you were before!

JANUARY

3

Allow yourself to say "no."

Give yourself a chance to say "no" or "later" before you say "yes." Though the cause may be a worthy one, your time, energy, resources, and emotions are limited. There's only so much you are able to take on at one time. Respect your personal limits by saying "yes" only when it's something you feel is right for you at this particular time.

4

Shift your focus.

Instead of measuring your lifestyle with that of the rich and famous, focus more on those less fortunate. As your gratitude for your own gifts grows, you'll find yourself less interested in comparing your life with the lives of others, and more inclined to share what you have with those in need...less apt to gaze at your neighbor's "greener grass," and more inspired to discover the blessings blooming all around you.

JANUARY

5

Tickle your funny bone.

Giggle, guffaw, chuckle, and snort (it's okay!).
Laughter brings out the kid in you as it washes
away the stress of the day. Humor is the best
antidote for tension, and also a sure-fire way to keep
things in perspective. No minor thing masquerading
as a major thing lasts long in the light of laughter!
Look for the humor hiding all around you.

6

An adventure is only an inconvenience
rightly considered.
G. K. Chesterton

When unexpected hurdles cross your path, you
have choices. You can stew over what might have
been, or give up the journey altogether. Or you can
work around or over the hurdles. Who knows what
practical lessons you'll learn, what needed strengths
you'll gain, and how much know-how you'll garner
from the experience? Hurdles are often God's way
of saying, "Hey, do it this way—for your own sake!"

JANUARY

7

A friend is a gift you give yourself.
Robert Louis Stevenson

Do yourself a favor: risk reaching out to a stranger. When you walk into a room, talk to someone you don't know yet rather than immediately gravitate to familiar faces. When a newcomer joins your group, be among the first to greet the person and let her know she's not only welcome, but important to you. You never know when you'll meet a "friend for life."

8

Stop and smell the cinnamon rolls.

Take time to savor your meals, beginning each one with a prayer of thanksgiving for the food in front of you. As you eat, take small bites and chew slowly. Note and enjoy the variety of flavors, textures, and aromas. This practice aids in digestion, and it helps you recognize more easily when you're full, so you'll eat only what you need.

JANUARY

9

*For peace of mind, resign as general
manager of the universe.*

The "lone hero" who single-handedly saves the day
is a myth! Not one of us succeeds without relying
on the skills, abilities, input, knowledge, advice,
experience, and presence of others. Open the way
for people around you to do their part, to help you
when and where they can, and to gain the pride and
confidence that comes with sharing their gifts with
others.

10

*I can't write a book commensurate with Shakespeare,
but I can write a book by me.*
Walter Raleigh

There's a difference between accepting reality and
settling for something you don't want. When you
consent to settle, you're taking the easy way out,
and giving up on yourself and your hopes and
dreams. But when you accept the reality of God-
given limitations and adjust your goals according-
ly, you're listening to God's will for your life and
following His way—the way to your true and
lasting happiness.

JANUARY

11

Knock down your own fences.

Do you ever feel you're "not enough"? Not pretty enough...witty enough...charming enough...smart enough? You fill in the blank! Negative statements you repeat to yourself can fence in your present and your future, because they highlight shortcomings instead of strengths (that is, if the statements are even true, which they're often not). Focus on what you are, because you're so much more than simply "enough"!

12

God didn't create anything without a purpose
(although mosquitoes come close).

In whatever happens, there's something to learn... even if it turns out to be, "I'll never do that again!" Your own challenges are what make you able to overcome adversity that comes into your life, figure out practical solutions to real-life problems, and empathize with others who are struggling. Ever realize how many times you've been able to help someone because you've come through the same thing?

13

No procrastination allowed!

Every woman faces tasks, decisions, or relationship issues she'd rather ignore. But ignoring something unpleasant doesn't cause it to disappear, but only lets it linger longer, perhaps intensify, and make life more stressful. Do yourself a favor today by doing one thing you've been putting off. Then you can give yourself a pat on the back for a job not only done, but well-done!

14

Genius is one percent inspiration
and 99 percent perspiration.
  Thomas Edison

It's said that Edison tried 10,000 ways to create the light bulb. Every failure taught him something that brought him closer to success, because he could eliminate one more way that didn't work. Though you may not need as many as 10,000 tries to reach your goal, don't give up! There's can-do in you that God can use to light your path ahead!

15

Zzzzz

A well-rested body is better prepared to face the mental, physical, and emotional challenges of a new day. During the day, schedule time out to replenish your energy by sitting quietly, or even taking a short nap, if possible. When evening arrives, follow a pleasant bedtime routine that is conducive to peaceful, restful, and sufficient sleep. Pamper yourself with a chance for sweet dreams.

16

Finish every day and be done with it.
You have done what you could.
      Ralph Waldo Emerson

At the end of the day, avoid second-guessing your every move. The day is over, and you can't go back and change a single thing about it! If there's something you should not have done, done better, or done differently for a more effective outcome, consider it a lesson learned. Make amends where you can, and then carry your new-found wisdom, not useless regrets, into tomorrow.

JANUARY

17

What had seemed easy in imagination was rather hard in reality.
Lucy Maud Montgomery

If your good plans aren't working out the way you had thought they would, maybe you need to go about them differently, or approach them from another direction. Perhaps there are tasks you can break down into smaller pieces, or a skill you need to acquire before going to the next phase. Ask God for guidance. He's the one who charted the path, so He knows the way.

18

Use the news.

Whether you hear, watch, or read the daily news, it can leave you feeling helpless. As much as you might want to, you can't save the world, but you can make positive changes. Volunteer your time, skills, and financial resources—your gifts make a difference. Pray that God will send help to those you're unable to reach. When you talk with others, choose to share "good" news.

19

Belief is a truth held in the mind; faith is a fire in the heart.
Joseph Fort Newton

Faith acts on what it believes, and acts with confidence. If the positive things you believe to be true about God, yourself, and others have no effect on your life, they're nothing more than feel-good thoughts. Faith on the inside acts on the outside. It's on display in the way you respond to others, regard your circumstances, and react to events in your life.

JANUARY

20

Send out an S.O.S.

Need help? Ask for it! Part of the joy of a relationship is being able to help another person, and very often someone's help is God's answer to your S.O.S. prayer. Where one person is weak, or stressed, or time-crunched, the other is capable, calm, and happy to lend you a hand. Your chance to answer another's S.O.S. will come soon enough.

21

Get to know your hero.

Describe the people you look up to as heroes, leaders, and role models. What about them inspires you, or has helped you become the person you are? Do a little digging. If you're acquainted with one of these people, ask questions. If he or she is a famous person, read a biography. Allow lessons they've learned increase your appreciation of them—and bring out the hero in you.

22

Time you enjoyed wasting is not wasted time.
Marthe Troly-Curtin

There's a time for hard work—a time to do everything you can to get things done—and there's a time to sit back and relax. Celebrate everything you've accomplished, and mark your progress on projects you have yet to complete. Congratulate yourself for sticking to it, despite the setbacks that have come your way. Dream! Bask in the beauty of a lazy day.

J ANUARY

23

*Worry is the interest paid on trouble
before it falls due.*
William Ralph Inge

"What if...?" That's how worry starts. It begins with
a niggling fear that something bad might happen,
and then it morphs into chronic worry that it
will happen! Stop wasting your time fretting about
tomorrow's troubles. God is on your side, and
He's by your side. He will see to it that you have
everything you need to handle whatever comes
into your life.

24

Make you life a mission, not an intermission.
Arnold H. Glasgow

How you spend your time every day is how you're
spending your life. Are you engaged in activities and
pursuits that matter, have meaning to you, and give
value to others? Think about the footprints you're
leaving behind for others to follow. Are you happy
with what they look like? Purposefully invest your
precious time, and yourself, in worthwhile things.

25

If the world seems cold to you,
kindle fires to warm it.
Lucy Larcom

Some days are just plain tough. Nothing you do seems to turn out right, and everyone you talk to seems out-of-sorts. If it's a cold and gray winter's day, that only adds to your misery! But you can reverse the trend. Save for tomorrow any task that can wait. Treat yourself to a mug of steaming coffee. And smile—it will brighten your day, and someone else's, too!

26

Plan your work, and then work your plan.

Of course you have a picture of the way you want things to turn out. Share your future with God, and then leave it in His hands, so you can focus on what He has put in your hands—today. Involve yourself fully in the day's needs and activities, tasks and responsibilities, and don't worry about the end result. Remember, it's in very capable hands!

27

Olly olly oxen free!

Do you hide behind a mask when you're around other people? Do you use jokes, silence, busyness, or even what you wear to camouflage the true you? Why? You're an original, a one-of-a-kind masterpiece! A copy, or a substitute, is never as amazing as the real thing. Do something today to reveal the real you. Come out of hiding!

28

If you're doing nothing but waiting for your ship to come in, you've already missed the boat!

Wouldn't it be nice if God would simply give you what you want right now, complete and entire? He has that kind of power. But the fact He isn't using it tells you something—such as, you have the ability to act, create, do, and make things happen. He's given you gifts He loves to see you use, and experiences He'd like you to have. What more could anyone ask?

JANUARY

29

Take yourself lightly.

Being able to laugh at yourself—without believing you're a joke—is a delicate balancing act. But it's one worth mastering, because it keeps things in perspective, strengthens relationships, and deals with life's faux pas and awkward situations in a healthy way. Give up trying to impress others, smile, and simply enjoy being you. It's the key to a "lighter" life.

30

Don't judge each day by the harvest you reap,
but by the seeds that you plant.
Robert Louis Stevenson

Every little thing you do for others matters, and you may never know how much. The card you send to a friend, the help you offer to a coworker, the smile you give to a stranger might be what makes that person's day—or week. It could be what prompts her to do the same for another, and another, and another. Make today count in lots of little, wonderful ways!

31

Let God be God.

Guess who's God? Yep, you're right. God is God, with all the strength, power, glory, wisdom, compassion, and love you can imagine, and then some. So why not gather up all those times you've thought you knew better than God? Take them to Him, have a good laugh with Him, and then let Him throw them away. Whew! Now you can be you, just the way He made you.

Remember,
you are
in His arms today...
and every day.

FEBRUARY

The Lord is the strength of my life;
of whom shall I be afraid?
Psalm 27:1

You know the people who will be there for you—those special family members, friends, and neighbors who are the first to ask if they can do anything to help. With every kind and thoughtful thing they do, you're reminded that you're never alone, and that whatever happens, they will not let you down.

But even more than the most faithful of friends is your ever-reliable God. You can lean on Him at any time, day or night, asking Him for strength, courage, increased faith, or just a whisper from Him to let you know He's by your side. When feelings of fear leave you shaking in your heels (or sneakers), recall the many times His presence has embraced your heart. Let God lift your mood...renew your confidence...restore your peace of mind.

This month, take a few extra minutes each day to remember God's strong, deep, and unchangeable love for you. No matter where life has taken you, He is there to protect you, comfort you, and guide you along His way. Picture yourself in His arms, because that's exactly where you are!

FEBRUARY

1

*It isn't so astonishing, the number of things
that I can remember, as the number of things
I can remember that aren't so.*
　　　　Mark Twain

Memory isn't a reliable reporter! Time, strong
emotions, or subsequent events can interweave fact
and fiction to the point it's hard to separate the
two. Always leave room for the chance that what
might upset you about a past event may not have
happened exactly as you think. Take disturbing
memories to God, and let them rest with Him.

2

*To avoid criticism, say nothing,
do nothing, be nothing.*
　　　　Aristotle

You can't please everybody. You know it's true, yet
it hurts when someone criticizes the way you look
or the way you do things. If the criticism is unhelp-
ful, unwarranted, or mean-spirited, forget it and go
on. God, the one who really counts, is the one who
knows you best. Let Him guide you in His way—the
way that is right, no matter what others may say.

3

Excellence is a moving target.
　　　　Saying

A toddler and an adult may both do their best at a
given task, but results will be far from identical! But
doing your best every day and at every stage in life
is the only road to excellence. With the knowledge,
skills, maturity, and opportunities you possess
today, do your best work, understanding full well
that tomorrow your best will be even better.

4

Better by far you should forget and smile,
than that you should remember and be sad.
    Christina Rossetti

When past hurts or regrets weigh you down, lighten your emotional baggage. That's right—imagine yourself unpacking a suitcase, pulling out each thing from the past that causes anger, resentment, or bitterness today. Grieve, forgive, make amends, and take to heart lessons learned. Now throw away the excess weight! Move on, refusing to drag the past along with you into the future.

5

Reflect less on your reflection.

A mirror can't show you who you really are. While you might notice what's "wrong" with you, people who really know you see what's right—your kindness and helpfulness, and your desire to grow spiritually and draw closer to God. The words of mature and trusted friends and family members provide a better reflection than any mirror could. Let your loved ones help you see the true you more clearly.

6

A statement once let loose cannot be caught
by four horses.
    Proverb

You have a unique perspective on the world, and that's why sharing your point of view is so valuable. Refuse to bury your opinions, even when you believe others might disagree. Yet with the privilege of speaking comes the responsibility of speaking respectfully, truthfully, and purposefully. And the obligation of listening attentively to others. Your voice, as well as theirs, deserves to be heard.

FEBRUARY

7

*All I have seen teaches me to trust the
Creator for all I have not seen.*
Ralph Waldo Emerson

The beauty, diversity, complexity, and meticulous
order of the natural world are reminders that there's
more to this life than what you can see with your
eyes. Open your spiritual eyes to God, whose Word
created the world and everything in it (including
you!). Offer Him a word of thanks and praise for
flowers...sunshine...stars...whatever you're seeing
right now! Embrace the wonder and mystery that
surround you today.

8

Be an arms-open-wide receiver.

It's humbling to be on the receiving end of a gift.
But the other side of being a gracious giver is being
a gracious receiver in return. It's part of the give and
take of healthy, lasting, and meaningful relationships. Allow others to bless your life with the gifts
they have to offer. Let them know how much you
appreciate what they give you and what they do—
and most of all, how much you appreciate them.

9

*Let us remember that within us
there is a palace of immense magnificence.*
Teresa of Avila

You are a spiritual person. Your longing for purpose, peace, and a life hereafter is real and necessary, just as your desire for food and water. Through
your longings, God reaches out to you. He leads
you to more fully realize the extent of His love for
you, the good plans He has for you, and the tender
heart He will turn toward you forever. In Him,
you're more than meets the eyes.

10

*Remember: Two days from today,
tomorrow will be yesterday.*

You may not be looking forward to tomorrow. Perhaps there's a burdensome obligation awaiting you, or a dreaded doctor's appointment, or a difficult confrontation you'd just as soon avoid. But that's tomorrow! Don't let it mess up today. With God's help (and He will help you—that's a promise), you'll do what needs to be done when the time comes.

11

*Wrinkles should merely indicate
where smiles have been.*
Mark Twain

Each stage of life carries its own challenges and opportunities, yet it's easy to focus on the former rather than the latter. No matter how many candles are on your birthday cake this year, highlight the happy memories you have made...the meaningful relationships you have with others...the wisdom you have gathered along the way. Welcome each age with gratitude for all that has passed and anticipation for all that lies ahead.

12

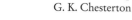

*Don't ever take a fence down until you know
the reason why it was put up.*
G. K. Chesterton

When other drivers follow the traffic laws, you're free to drive safely and confidently down the highway. Similarly, wise, judicious rules don't hinder freedom, but allow it to flourish. God's rules, too, keep you free *from* what would threaten, harm, or injure you, both spiritually and physically; and keep you free *for* fulfillment, joy, and peace of mind and heart. If you want to be free, let God's rules rule your life.

FEBRUARY

13

*Choose your battles
(and your swimsuits) wisely!*

There are some things worth fighting for, even dying for. But before you throw yourself into battle—whether it's with words or actions, thoughts or resources—weigh what's at stake. Most often, "winning" an argument or proving a point is not worth a broken relationship. Sometimes "principle" is more accurately termed "opinion." Make sure it's a battle worth the struggle before you engage in it.

14

God is love.
1 John 4:8

To love without expecting anything in return doesn't mean inviting others to walk all over you. It simply means continuing to give your best, even when others sometimes fail to respond in kind. Love that doesn't keep score is love in the truest sense of the word—and it's the kind of love God has for you. It's marked by forgiveness, understanding, compassion, and a willingness to go forward—in love.

15

By crawling a child learns to stand.
Proverb

Getting good at anything begins with baby steps—learning the basics, practicing regularly, gaining confidence, and even fumbling and stumbling along the way. Keep going! Whatever your aim—increased physical strength, proficiency at work, mastery of a skill, or deeper spiritual understanding—perseverance is the only way to achieve what you have in mind. The old saying, "Rome wasn't built in a day," is true!

FEBRUARY

16

*Reading is to the mind what
exercise is to the body.*
Joseph Addison

A good book is like a personal trainer for your
mind. It gives your imagination a workout, stretches
your vocabulary, and strengthens your focus and
concentration. The best book of all—the Bible—does
even more: it nourishes your soul and enlightens
your spirit with God's life-giving Word. Every day,
spend time in the company of books that are worth
your time and attention.

17

*You can grow separately without
growing apart.*

Whether it's your best friend, your children, or your
spouse, sharing life together is an immeasurable joy.
Ultimately, though, each person has his or her own
life to live. Hold your loved ones close, pray for
them and their needs, and let your presence in their
lives be a blessing to them. Enfold them in your
heart, all the while making sure everyone (including
you) has room to breathe.

FEBRUARY

18

*Good judgment comes from experience,
and experience—well, that comes from
poor judgment.*

At the very least, mistakes are embarrassing. Who wants to admit being taken in by a scam, duped by a stranger, or making an ill-considered choice? But lessons learned in the school of hard knocks are lessons well-learned. They increase awareness, so you are unlikely to "bite" next time (perhaps getting involved in something with far worse consequences); and they teach empathy for others caught in similar situations.

19

*A time to get, and a time to lose;
a time to keep, and a time to cast away.*
Ecclesiastes 3:6

What time is it for you? All life flows in cycles, stages, and seasons. You are not the person you were ten or five years ago, or even one year ago—and neither are the people around you. Circumstances, too, change with time. Don't fear letting go of attitudes, expectations, and even dreams and goals that no longer reflect who you are. What worked well for you yesterday may need revising or tossing today.

20

*Many want to serve God,
but only as advisors.*

God gave you reason for a reason! With what lies
between your ears, you can encounter your world,
figure things out, and grow in practical experience
and expertise. But there's something He didn't give
you, and that's the ability to know everything—past,
present, and future events in their entirety; the logic
behind each circumstance and situation; the inner
thoughts and motivations of others. Be spiritually
reasonable. Let Him lead.

21

There's no need to outsource your insight.

Woman's intuition is more than a gut feeling or
good guess. Your intuition is your earned wisdom,
your practical experience, and spiritual perception
all working in sync to send you a message. Listen to
it when it tugs at your mind or nudges at the edge
of your thoughts. Give yourself the time you need
to acknowledge it, explore it, and pray about it.
Then, act on it.

22

Sweep the skeletons out of your closet.

No bones about it, dark secrets can eat away at
your peace of mind. Ask God for the courage,
strength, and determination to bring them into
the clear light of day relying on Him for complete
forgiveness. Share what burdens your heart with a
trusted Christian mentor who can help you make
amends where needed. Once secrets are exposed,
they're more easily disposed.

23

Few things help an individual more than to place responsibility upon him and let him know that you trust him.
Booker T. Washington

"I'd rather do it myself!" You can do it faster and better, and have it done just the way you want it. But delegating tasks to others is both wise and kind. It frees your time, and it gives others the chance to shine and grow, and to have purpose and be productive. Very often, the hands of others are the hands God gives you so you can fulfill all that He has in mind for you.

24

Opportunity may knock once, but temptation bangs on your door forever.

Each one of us has a weak spot—or maybe several! It's the one, two, or three things we shouldn't do and don't want to do, but do anyway. Even if we manage to stop, the inclination lingers like an unwanted guest. Whenever temptation calls, call on God. His strength is your shield, His arm your support, and His love your assurance of compassion, forgiveness, and power to follow His will.

FEBRUARY

25

Dost thou love life? Then do not squander time,
for that's the stuff life is made of.
Benjamin Franklin

When you give your time to people and to pursuits, you're giving your life. The same is true of those who give their time to you. Remember what a priceless and irreplaceable gift time is, and use yours in worthwhile, life-building, and joy-giving ways. Show others that you value the gift of their time when they spend it with you. Receive time and use time with attentiveness and appreciation.

26

Mix a little foolishness with your serious plans:
it's lovely to be silly at the right moment.
Horace

Sometimes, it's when you're right in the middle of a tense or serious situation that you need a touch of something not-so-serious, like a stress-relieving witticism, a smile-creating quip, a lighthearted insight. You don't need to be an accomplished comedian, just someone willing to look beyond the stark, bare facts and see another fact—there's a silly side to many serious things. To get in practice, think of something you "seriously" stressed over that came out fine. Don't waste energy needlessly—and don't take your self too seriously.

27

*Happy people are those who can enjoy
the scenery while on a detour.*

When your day heads in a direction different than
the one you had planned, don't miss the scenery
along the way. Keep your eyes, ears, and heart open
for unexpected opportunities that may appear just
around the corner. Be prepared to discover surprising
beauty and unforeseen blessings in the twists
and turns of real-life events. Your "way off track"
could be God's "right on track" for you.

28

*Don't miss the donut by looking
through the hole.*

It's only natural to focus on the problem—that's
what needs to be fixed, right? But dwelling on a
particular problem blows it out of proportion,
to the point the problem is all you see and think
about. Ironically, intense attention to a problem
most often hides the solution! Balance your thinking
and your perspective by putting today's problem
alongside all the blessings you possess right now. It
looks pretty small, doesn't it? Small enough to fix.

FEBRUARY

If it's Leap Year, you have an extra day
to celebrate a lovely month!

29

Time is the wisest of all counselors.
     Plutarch

Every four years you get a bonus day. Why not
use it in gratitude for all that time has brought
you? Over the years, you've gained wisdom and
discernment—increased knowledge of yourself,
other people, and God. In so many ways, God
uses time to bless you with deeper and deeper
spiritual insights so you can know Him better
and love Him more. And all the time, He knows
and loves you completely!

Some people,
like angels,
leave a hint
of heaven
wherever
they go.

MARCH

Be kind and compassionate to one another.
Ephesians 4:32 NIV

You probably will never forget the people who treat you with kindness and consideration. Their thoughtfulness lingers in the heart, and the warmth and acceptance you feel around them makes you want to be—where else?—around them! People are drawn to people, who, like angels, care for others and care about others in visible, practical ways.

Unlike money, fame, or status, kindness is within reach of anyone who wants it. All it takes is daily determination to act considerately toward others (yes, even that irritating coworker who sits next to you). It takes attentiveness (despite your personal problems) to see the elderly woman struggling to reach an item on the highest shelf in the grocery aisle...the young mother with three toddlers in tow trying to open a door...the teen who's desperate for someone to listen and to care.

This month, give special thanks to the kind and caring angels in your life—those who leave a hint of heaven wherever they go. Renew, restore, and nurture the angel in you with countless acts of kindness to others.

MARCH

1

Wherever you are, be all there.
Jim Elliott

Whether you're in a time of abundance or need, celebration or sorrow, today comes around only once. Refuse to put yourself on autopilot. Notice the colors, textures, and sounds around you. See—really see—the people you meet, because that's the only way you'll notice who needs an angel in their life today. And then stop and be that special angel.

2

I am fearfully and wonderfully made.
Psalm 139:14

Consider the intricate miracle of the body and brain you have the privilege of possessing and using each day. Ponder each breath—inhale, exhale!—each heartbeat, each movement of hands and arms, legs and toes. Rejoice in the ability to think, dream, imagine, hope, reason, feel, and believe. Be kind and gentle in the way you treat yourself, because you're an extraordinary piece of God's handiwork!

3

Character is what you are in the dark.
Dwight L. Moody

A woman of integrity is the same person in front of an audience that she is when no one's watching. Speaking and acting with the same measure of kindness, understanding, and respect in private as you would in public lets the true you shine through. What's more, you won't have to worry about blurting out what you think when you're in the habit of thinking kind and loving thoughts!

MARCH

4

*A gossip always gets caught in
her own mouth-trap.*

Gone are the days when gossip passed from neighbor to neighbor across back fences of small towns. Now all it takes is a tap on the "send" button to spread the salacious details around the world. Though you can't stop others from passing on hurtful stories about friends and coworkers, you can delete them from your email—and your mind. When it comes to gossip, you can show by word and action that "the story stops here."

5

With each sunrise, we start anew.

No matter what happened yesterday or the day before, today is a new day. It's another chance to make choices that really matter, such as the choice to rely on God for wisdom and guidance...ignore real or perceived slights...speak words of comfort, healing, and affirmation...laugh and love life for no other reason than because you can. Every day, it's your personal, individual, God-given choice.

6

Friends are kisses blown to us by angels.

Friends move in and out of your life as addresses change, opportunities emerge, and interests intersect, and then drift in opposite directions. Yet that doesn't make the friends you have made along the way obsolete. They're still people who have played a part in your life and in your heart. Why not reconnect with an old friend today? That you remember—and care—could be the best thing that has happened to someone in a long time.

7

No answer is also an answer.
Proverb

Unanswered questions are a part of everyone's life, particularly in the area of faith. Don't let what you don't know about God, His ways, and the mysteries of the universe keep you on the spiritual sidelines. Believe in and act on what God has said about Himself: He created you with a plan and a purpose, He loves you, and He is present in your life. Trust that God, all-wise and all-knowing, holds the answers to all the rest.

8

No one is perfect;
that's why pencils have erasers.
Proverb

Giving your all in everything you do is an admirable trait. Expecting perfection, though, is something else again—impossible! Treat yourself kindly when you come face to face with the fact you're not perfect. Refuse to mentally beat yourself up when things don't go as planned, or you fall short of your expectations. Sincerely say "I forgive you," just as you would to anyone you love.

9

It's never too late to be what
you might have been.
George Eliot

All right, maybe it's too late to become a prima ballerina or star hockey player, but it's not too late to live your dream. If you're not on stage or in the field, cheer on those who are. Nothing beats the bravos of an enthusiastic audience! If the goal you had set your heart on is closed to you, open your heart to caring, supporting, and encouraging. You may discover it's the most rewarding place to be of all!

MARCH

10

Just because the shoe fits,
you don't have to buy it.

Being content with what you have is a wonderfully stress-free way to live. It's also kind to your bank account! Cultivate the habit of planned and purposeful shopping, buying what you really need and truly want at the best price and quality available to you. That way, you're more likely to feel good about your purchases, and have money left over to share with others and help meet their needs.

11

Time is a very precious gift of God;
so precious that it's only given to us
moment by moment.
Amelia Barr

You are an interesting woman. Even when you're alone, there's no reason for you to feel lonely. Use the time to get to know yourself! There's always more you can discover, dream about, and find pleasure in doing. Draw, write, putter in the garden, talk a walk, or sit by a window and watch the clouds float by. Be an angel to yourself by becoming your own good company.

12

A woman of words and not of deeds
is like a garden full of weeds.
Author Unknown

If you don't like the direction your life is headed, change it. What have you been promising yourself you'll do "someday"? What have you mentioned to friends that you'd like to accomplish? Today, take a practical step toward getting there. Become the woman, wife, mother, daughter, aunt, friend you want to be. Rewrite your story, and let your "happily ever after" begin now.

MARCH

13

*Only those who risk going too far can
possibly find out how far one can go.*
　　　　T. S. Eliot

Push beyond the physical, mental, emotional, and
spiritual boundaries you usually live within. Ask
more of yourself, because you're stronger, smarter,
and more deeply loved than you could ever imagine.
Ask more of God, too—ask Him to reveal Himself
to you, to make you aware of His presence in your
day and His plan for your life. Risk following Him,
and discover a world of infinite joy and love.

14

Love is the beauty of the soul.
　　　　Augustine

If you've been hurt by someone you love, it's possible that you're very wary of loving again. Will you
face the loss of another relationship? You know,
maybe you will; there are no assurances in love, as
in life. But life without love is like a day without
sunshine. Today, turn to God, whose love never
changes, and ask Him to help you learn to love
again.

MARCH

15 *Give first impressions a second chance.*

It's said that first impressions are lasting impressions, but it doesn't have to be true for you. A poor first impression can turn you away from opportunities, interests, experiences—even people—that are well worth a second look. Before jumping to conclusions, think about what you saw or heard, and ask yourself if you might have missed something. You have more to gain than to lose by giving them another try.

16 *A good example is always the best sermon and the most effective teacher.*

What you do speaks louder than what you say. Encourage others toward positive change in attitude and action by practicing what you preach—and you won't have to preach at all! In the same way, look at others whose conduct and achievements you admire, and emulate them. Be a good example to others, and choose good examples for yourself so you can reach your highest potential.

MARCH

17

He maketh me to lie down in green pastures.
Psalm 23:2

Getaway vacations promise rest and relaxation,
and often that's what they deliver—along with fun,
laughter, and memory-making times. But for real
rest, you need go no further than God, whose Holy
Spirit lives in you. Let your body and mind relax in
knowing He is there for you—always. Let your heart
trust in His power. Let Him nourish your soul in
the green pastures of His love for you.

18

From a shy, timid girl I had become
a woman of resolute character,
who could no longer be frightened
by the struggle with troubles.
Anna Dostoevsky

Being a self-assured woman begins with being self-
aware. Take an objective inventory of your strengths
and weaknesses so you can be honest about what
you can and cannot do. In areas where you would
like to build skill and expertise, learn from those
who are willing and able to teach you. Tomorrow
you could be a little stronger, a little wiser, and a
little braver than you are today.

MARCH

19 *Cooperation is doing with a smile*
what you have to do anyway.
Author Unknown

Teamwork takes cooperation and delegation.
No one can do it all! Perform your part well by
going about it with a positive attitude. Be generous
with your help, willing to share your knowledge,
ideas, and expertise with everyone else on the
team—whether your "team" consists of family, club
members, special interest associates, or a workplace
group. View your team as a body, each part of it
working toward mutual good health and emotional
well-being.

20 *I'll tell you how the sun rose a ribbon at a time.*
Emily Dickinson

Twice a day, weather permitting, the sky becomes
an artist's canvas. If you're a morning person, make
a special point to look or go outside and savor the
sunrise. If you're a night person, set aside time and
make a date with the sunset. Offer the Creator
thanks for the beauty of His work—sunrise, sunset,
trees, flowers, mountains, hills, valleys, brooks,
lakes, and seas. Appreciate the world you live in.

21

I make the most of all that comes
and the least of all that goes.
Sara Teasdale

Before you go to sleep, prayerfully put "today" to bed. Celebrate the blessings you have received, and thank God for the special people who have stepped into your life this day. Ask His forgiveness for your failings, and then let them go; give over any worries into His capable hands. Refuse to regret your losses, but sleep peacefully, looking forward to a new day filled with beauty, abundance, and love.

22

Kindness is like a boomerang—
it always comes back to you.

When you put your comfort and convenience aside for the sake of another's need, you're a special angel in that person's life. When you give of your resources, time, energy, and expertise to fill someone else's lack, what you get back in gratitude, good feelings, and heartfelt appreciation far surpasses anything you have given. Whenever you give of yourself, it's win-win all around.

MARCH

23

Be a "Wait" Watcher.

God's timing can differ widely from human timing!
While you wait for His answers to your prayers,
watch. Watch for signs of His work in your life.
Look for openings and opportunities, as well as
changes in your thinking and in how you see your
circumstances. Be aware of the people around you,
of what they say and do, for many are angels in
disguise. Yes, God answers prayer. While you work
toward your heart's desire, wait on God—and watch.

24

*Be kind, for everyone you meet is
fighting a hard battle.*
Ian MacLaren

The driver who cuts you off...the clerk who is
short with you...the friend who seems to look right
through you...how easy to make a snap judgment
about their "problem"! But you never know what's
going on behind the scenes...what you can't see...
what isn't evident at first sight. The benefit of the
doubt is a precious gift, along with a gentle word
and an understanding smile.

25

*Patience is bitter,
but its fruit is sweet.*
Proverb

Fast planes, microwaves, overnight delivery,
email, text messages..."instant" is pretty much
the expected speed for today's society. And why
shouldn't it be? We can get what we want when
we want it! But for things of lasting value, nature's
a more realistic model. Learn from the passing
seasons, each with its own rhythm, beauty, and
purpose. Patience yields the sweetest fruit in the
orchard—and in life.

MARCH

26 *Celebrate the wonders of womanhood.*

Being a woman opens your life to distinctive
challenges, but also to unique blessings. Learn how
courageous women who have gone before you have
met the challenges of their day, and give thanks
for the countless blessings you enjoy because of
their influence. Celebrate what's fantastic about
femininity. Refuse to accept stereotypes about
women or men, and instead honor both as God's
good gifts to one another.

27 *Compliments, like casseroles,*
are best served warm.

If you admire a woman's shoes or like her outfit, tell
her, right then and there (unless, of course, she's in
the middle of a speech!). The same goes for anything
else she does or is. Consciously look for something
positive and uplifting about everyone you meet, and
let genuine, heartfelt compliments flow easily from
your lips. You know how good it feels to receive
them yourself (and you will).

28 *A boggled mind equals a humbled heart.*

Not everything that happens to you or to anyone
else can be explained through science, human experience, and the laws of nature. Instead of fearing the
unexplainable, highlight it. Celebrate it. Let it open
your eyes to the amazing, extraordinary, unexpected, and divine side of the universe and of humanity.
Your heart can easily embrace the wonder, wisdom,
and knowledge that your mind can't fully grasp.

MARCH

29

He shall give his angels charge over thee.
Psalm 91:11

When bad things happen, you might wonder where God's angels are! Aren't they supposed to protect you and keep you safe? Yes—and they do. Even when hardships enter your life, you can trust that His angels are there to help you come through with your faith intact, and even strengthened. Though invisible, angels work through the voices, hearts, and hands of those who walk along with you.

30

No one can make you feel inferior without your consent.
Eleanor Roosevelt

No one (except God) knows you better than you. You know when you are giving your best effort, doing your best work, reaching for your best self. Though the true angels in your life will offer helpful advice and constructive criticism, some people will try to belittle your ambitions or dismiss your work. Don't let their comments deter you. Only you can say how far you've come or how far you have to go.

31

I am a little pencil in the hand of a writing God, who is sending a love letter to the world.
Mother Teresa

Your "letter to the world" is written one day at a time. It's not on paper or computer screen, but its words are spelled out every time you speak, and what you really mean is illustrated by every action you take. Your "letter" will not reach the whole world, but it will reach your corner of it, opened and read by those whose lives you touch today. What kind of "letter" will it be?

God cares about
the BIG things,
the small things,
and All things
in your life.

APRIL

I have called you friends.
John 15:15

You've probably heard or read about people who have survived a harrowing experience. Very often, they will thank God for giving them hope, encouraging them along the way, and seeing them through. Perhaps you can recall feeling the strong and comforting hand of God hold you up during a particularly difficult time.

But what about all those other times—when everyday frustrations mount and relatively minor concerns threaten your peace of mind? Those are times when your all-seeing, all-knowing heavenly Father opens His arms to you. Nothing you experience is too ordinary, too small, or too mundane to take to God in prayer. If it's big enough to trouble you in any way, it's big enough to share with God.

Remember, God is God, but He is also your friend. You can talk to Him about whatever is on your mind or burdens your heart. Just as your body naturally desires food and water, your soul craves the nourishment only He can give. Take everything to God—He cares. He hears. He acts.

APRIL

1

Be happy. It's one way of being wise.
Colette

There's a little girl in you who understands the power of pure delight...the cleansing laughter of a goofy comedy or a silly joke...the pleasure of watching, as if for the first time, a butterfly alighting on the petal of a newly opened blossom. Smile, giggle, sing, dance, and clap your hands with glee! When you look for joy, you find it. No fooling!

2

Everybody needs beauty as well as bread, places to play in and pray in, where nature may heal and give strength to body and soul.
John Muir

All creation is a glorious gallery of God's handiwork! Look around you, from the changing tides to the setting sun...wildflowers to wildebeests...wispy clouds to desert sands...soaring birds to a woodland stream lazily making its way along its meandering course. No matter where you are, you're surrounded by marvelous works of art. Take time today to see and appreciate nature. And why not offer a word of "thanks" to the Master Artist, too?

A P R I L

3

You must do the thing you think you cannot do.
Eleanor Roosevelt

Everyone has fears, both big and small. Who knows when, or if ever, you'll come face-to-face with yours? Instead of letting your imagination keep you in constant dread of the day, acknowledge your fears. Try to determine what might lie at the heart of them. Take anything that you're afraid of and hand it over to God—with His strength to rely on, there's nothing you can't overcome.

4

Could we change our attitude,
we should not only see life differently,
but life itself would come to be different.
Katherine Mansfield

If you're feeling irritated or indifferent toward the people you live or work with, refuse to act on your emotions. Instead, choose to pay a compliment... speak an encouraging word...offer to help them with a task...spend time listening to what they have to say. Not only will your actions change your mood for the better, it will sweeten the atmosphere and lift the spirits of those around you, too.

APRIL

5

Whatsoever things are true, whatsoever things are honest, whatsoever things are just, whatsoever things are pure, whatsoever things are lovely, whatsoever things are of good report...think on these things.
Philippians 4:8

Your thoughts are the soundtrack of your life. If you don't like what's playing, change the channel immediately! Focus on the positive aspects of who you are, where you are, and what you're doing. Expose any hurtful lies you keep repeating to yourself, and refuse to dwell on the real or imagined shortcomings of others. Revel in the truth.

6

A misty morning doesn't signify a cloudy day.
Proverb

When facing an uphill battle, things might look pretty overwhelming from where you stand. But you're not seeing the full picture of what the future holds. In fact, no one can from any vantage point— no one, that is, except God. He knows the blessings He has in store for you...blessings far more delightful and abundant than you can imagine. So hang in there. Change is in the air!

APRIL

7

Lighten your load!

Just as a lot of little worries can keep you on edge, household clutter can make you feel constantly overwhelmed. It's time for spring cleaning! Focus on the small stuff. Tackle one drawer, one closet, one cupboard; then the next. Organize what you want to keep, donate usable items, and toss the rest. The more in control your surroundings are, the more in control you'll feel about your life.

8

One day is worth two tomorrows.
Benjamin Franklin

It's a good day—make the most of it! If you're busy, revel in the ability to think, do, and achieve... if you don't have anything special going on, use your God-given time to savor the sights and sounds around you...if you're striving, attaining, or recovering from illness, rejoice in the fact that you're further along today than yesterday...and remember: today and every day, you're in God's good, strong, gentle, and capable hands.

9

A wisdom break prevents mistakes.

You possess knowledge—you've been to school, you've had experiences (both good and bad), you've seen a slice of life. But wisdom is different. With wisdom, you know what to do with what you know. For big decisions and small ones, major choices and minor ones, speeches in front of many and a whisper to a single person, take a moment to think before you act. It turns knowledge into wisdom.

10

Let us accept the truth,
even when it surprises us and alters our views.
George Sand

Truth can't be squeezed, halved, or stretched! What is, is. Period. Whether the matter is significant or not, get in the habit of telling the truth in the kindest possible way, in line with the facts. Avoid little white lies, because they rarely remain little for long. Your consistent truth-telling (even when it's not flattering to you) assures those around you that they can trust your words—and your character.

11

A pint can't hold a quart—if it holds a pint,
it is doing all that can be expected of it.
Margaret Deland

Before committing to spend your time, money, or energy in a big way, stop and consider the big picture—specifically, your calendar...your budget...your health. Be realistic about how much you have to offer, and acknowledge the emotional toll that might be involved or the stress that comes with having too much going on at one time. Don't spend, give, or promise more than you have—of anything.

12

Community is the place where God completes our lives with His joy.
Henri Nouwen

God created you to be a loved, lovable, and loving woman...to love and be loved in return. Whether it's your friends, family, neighbors, coworkers, or church, those close to you are there to receive your love...and you are there to offer them yours. Miss no opportunity to spend time with others, even if it's only a few minutes to chat. Their love enriches your life, as your love enriches theirs.

13

Winter is what makes spring so sweet.

It's easy to take for granted something you enjoy all the time. When worry, illness, or accidents come, things like peace of mind, good health, and the ease of an ordinary day emerge as the great blessings they really are! Today, let spring's blossoms remind you that winter has passed, and so will the day's problems and burdens. Ask God to strengthen your faith, hope, and certainty in His promises.

14

A full schedule doesn't make for a full life.

Ultimately, it's time with people—listening, talking, sharing, helping, giving, receiving—that makes for a full and satisfying life. Without strong, meaningful, and lasting relationships of many kinds (including a vibrant relationship with God), activities, acquisitions, credentials, wealth, and possessions count for nothing. If you're too busy to build and nurture your relationships, you're too busy. What can you do to make room for the people around you?

APRIL

15

*The most powerful weapon on Earth
is the human soul on fire.*
Ferdinand Foch

What you truly care about, you do something
about. And the best "something" is more than simply spouting off to anyone who will listen! If there's
a cause or situation that sets your blood boiling,
put that heat to effective use. Write well-thought-
out letters to influential people. Give your time and
resources to help turn things around. Join other
like-minded people in making the changes you want
to see.

16

*It isn't difficult to make a mountain out
of a molehill—just add a little dirt.*
Author Unknown

Not all bumps in the road are more than simply
that—bumps. When there's a hurdle in your path,
look at it objectively so you can plan how to jump
over it or go around it. Don't let fear make it more
formidable than it really is! Expend the time,
attention, effort, resources, and emotional energy
that each problem warrants. Give no less, but no
more, either.

APRIL

17

Spend all you have for loveliness.
Sara Teasdale

Want to enjoy a lovely life? Then be lovely. How? Not by raiding the cosmetics counter at your local department store, but by using words that encourage, build up, inspire, and motivate...by perceiving the loveliness of those around you and appreciating the best of every situation...by shaping your actions to convey peace, gentleness, acceptance, and respect for others. That's the kind of loveliness that will never fade with time.

18

You're not obligated to fix everything that's broken.

When a friend shares a problem with you, ask if she'd like to hear your thoughts before offering suggestions on how to fix her problem. Very often, friends just need to express how they're feeling with someone they trust, and in doing so, they find the solution that's right for them and their circumstances. Listening is helping—and never forget that God is always there to listen to you, whatever the issue.

19

Resolve to be thyself.
Matthew Arnold

There never has been, and there never will be, another you. Your smile, your personality, your gifts, and your love can change the world for the better each day. Believe that the world's more beautiful because of you, and it will be. Know that even little things count—a helpful gesture here, an encouraging word there—because they do. They do to you, don't they? Then they do to others, as well.

APRIL

20

Walk a mile in her stilettoes before you judge.

Everyone's life is a mix of blessings and hardships, gifts and shortcomings, failures and successes. All you can read from where you stand is the cover blurb of another woman's life. You never know what big challenges she's struggling with right now, or what little things keep her up at night like a swarm of hungry mosquitoes. There's always more to her story—and to yours—than meets the eye.

21

There's no place like home...really.

No matter how long you've lived at your present address, there's always more to discover. Why not take a walk around your neighborhood and purposefully seek out something new? Or venture down an alleyway that has long intrigued you, but you've always been "too busy" to explore? Or find out more about the history of the place at the library or local museum? Discover what sets your corner of the world apart from the rest.

22

There is only one happiness in life,
to love and be loved.
George Sand

A few simple words can pack a lot of power! Those words are as simple as, "I love you." Sure, your family and friends know you love them, mostly by the way you treat them and care about them in real and practical ways. But there's still something powerful about saying "I love you" out loud. Those words are a gift that's a joy to both give and receive. Give them away today.

APRIL

23

You are younger today than you ever will be again.
Make use of it for the sake of tomorrow.
Author Unknown

What have you done different lately? If the answer is "not much," shake up your daily routine by trying something new. It doesn't have to be wild and crazy, just new to you. Prepare a recipe that recently caught your eye. Taste a food you've always wanted to try. Read a book outside your usual genre. Try on an outfit you'd usually pass by. A few new favorites might be awaiting your discovery!

24

God tells us to burden Him with
whatever burdens us.

It might be one huge issue or a hundred small ones—either way, you feel overburdened and overstressed. Your whole body knows when it happens! So breathe—literally. Give yourself a break by closing your eyes and breathing deeply for a few moments. Then deliver your worries, your tiredness, and your anxiety to God in prayer. Now you're ready to start again and do what needs to be done.

25

Have patience with all things,
but chiefly have patience with yourself.
Francis de Sales

You're a smart, intelligent woman—and that has nothing to do with diplomas or degrees, but everything to do with being you. But in every life, God permits certain weaknesses, yet always for a reason and with a purpose. The more familiar you are with your shortcomings, the more readily you'll ask God for help in overcoming them, and experience the strength and confidence that come from meeting challenges face-to-face.

A P R I L

26

*If you ever find happiness by hunting for it,
you will find it, as the old woman did her lost
spectacles, safe on her nose all the time.*
Josh Billings

Sure, there are happy places and not-so-happy
places where you may find yourself. Yet lasting
happiness depends more on a frame of mind than
on a place or circumstance. If you want to be happy,
simply be happy—here and now. Your smile will
make you feel good, and you can take it with you
wherever you go. What's more, it will warm the
hearts of others who haven't learned the happiest
(and no-cost) way of being happy.

27

Weigh who's leading the way.

Whose example and advice do you follow? Whose
attitudes and opinions inform yours? Before you
follow them and before you adopt their ways,
observe their actions...think through what they
say...see if their experience and expertise match the
position of influence you're giving them. Only those
who are worthy of your time and attention, respect
and admiration, will lead you along the right path.

28

*Write injuries in sand,
kindnesses in marble.*
Proverb

Both forgiveness and appreciation are within your
power to give. Offer both generously, even if you
don't receive the same in return. When you do,
you're doing it God's way, because He is quick to
forgive and eager to bless. He forgets your shortcomings and supports your efforts to change for the
better through the gift of His Spirit living in you. Is
there someone you have the honor of forgiving or
appreciating today?

29

Dress yourself from the inside-out.

Clothes don't "make the woman." They don't have that kind of power, no matter who designed them or how much they cost. Who you are, not what you wear, is your true source of beauty. Though stylish and attractive clothes may make a good impression, it's the words you use, the attitude you convey, and the things you do that make a lasting impression. Check your heart, as well as the mirror, as you dress each morning.

30

Miss no single opportunity of making some small sacrifice, here by a smiling look, there by a kindly word; always doing the smallest right and doing it all for love.

Thérèse of Lisieux

It's easy to dismiss all the little ways to show care for others because, well, they're little. Yet when you think how much someone's smile of welcome warmed your heart...how a friend's gentle hug comforted you...how a greeting from a stranger made you feel noticed and respected...then you know how big those little things really are. God knows, too, and that's why He cares about every itty-bitty thing about you.

If you want
to know
what heaven
looks like,
make someone
smile.

M A Y

The cheerful heart has a continual feast.
Proverbs 15:15 NIV

The power of a smile is hard to overestimate. It lifts your mood when you're feeling down...chases away negative thoughts when they threaten your peace of mind...smoothes relationships when they get a little frayed at the edges...sends a signal to others that you feel good about yourself, and that means you're more than likely to feel good about them, too.

A smile exudes confidence and projects understanding and caring. If you're going through a tough time, it reminds you of the many blessings in your life. A smile invites sharing and conversation, and opens the way to friendship and meaningful ties between people. If you would like to encourage yourself and be an encourager to others, an easy and relaxed smile will get you going immediately.

This month, experience the power of a smile. You'll be surprised at what a smile can do for you, and amazed at the difference it makes in your relationships with others. What's more, a smile is the simplest (and cheapest) way to get an instant face lift!

M A Y

1

*Cheerfulness keeps up a kind of daylight
in the mind, and fills it with a steady
and perpetual serenity.*
Joseph Addison

No one is happy all the time, day in and day out.
There are times when there's little to be happy
about! Yet adversity, met with hope and optimism,
is easier to bear. A cheerful attitude provides practical, real-life perspective, reminding you that tough
times don't last forever. Your determination not to
let your circumstances define you is evident in the
warmth of your smile, words, and actions.

2

*Voyage, travel, and change of
place impart vigor.*
Seneca

If you need a vacation but can't get away, take a
mental flight of fancy. Read up on a city or country
you'd like to visit someday. Learn something new
about the people, history, culture, language, traditions, music, or food. Note sites you're particularly
interested in seeing. Maybe even prepare a meal
based on their style of cooking. Savor the seasonings...and the anticipation of going there!

MAY

3

*When good cheer is lacking,
our friends will be packing.*

Who wants to hang out with a negative person? No one—yet it's often impossible to avoid dealing with them. When you approach unpleasant people with warmth and a smile, however, you protect yourself from their pessimism and defuse their destructive attitude. Your consistent confidence and cheerfulness lets them know that you're not interested in being miserable—and shows them how to take life with a smile.

4

*A woman's hopes are woven of sunbeams;
a shadow annihilates them.*
George Eliot

You may not be able to prevent fearful thoughts from entering your mind, but you have the power to send them right out again. You're not required to entertain unfounded scenarios where everything bad that can happen, happens! Instead, separate vague fears from realistic cautions; you can handily dismiss the former, giving you freedom to focus on the latter effectively and with a clear, untroubled mind.

MAY

5

Many men go fishing all of their lives without knowing that it is not fish they are after.
Henry David Thoreau

What puts you in touch with your heart's deepest feelings? Perhaps it's a quiet morning stroll or an afternoon spent puttering in the garden...listening to a piece of music or reading a book of poetry... visiting an art museum or writing in your journal. The more time you can hear what your heart has to say, the better you will know yourself...and what it is you truly want to do at this stage of your life.

6

Pray without ceasing.
1 Thessalonians 5:17

Worry is a thought that's headed in the wrong direction! It's focused inward, putting the entire burden on you to fix, change, and solve the problem. Instead, send your worries upward and give God your worries. Do what's within your power to do, and let God handle the rest by turning whatever fills your heart and mind with worry into a prayer of trust and thanksgiving.

M A Y

7

Humor is mankind's greatest blessing.
Mark Twain

Make *yourself* smile! Or maybe it's better said,
let yourself smile. A miss or mess-up may cause a
moment of embarrassment, but once you've gained
everything it can teach you for next time, laugh it
off! If others laugh at you, laugh with them. There's
no better way to show that you don't take yourself
so seriously that you can't enjoy God's good gift of
laughter—even if it's at your own expense.

8

She gives double who gives unasked.
Proverb

Choose to live a bit below your means. That way,
you'll always have a financial cushion to soften
the blow of an unexpected car repair or appliance
breakdown. Also, you'll be able to give more generously and spontaneously when a friend is walking
for a cause you care about...your church is holding a
benefit dinner...your favorite charity is having a fund
drive. It's giving that keeps you smiling all over!

9

Nothing is better than simplicity.
Walt Whitman

Sometimes life gets so cluttered with must-dos and must-haves that it's difficult to really enjoy anything. Perhaps not one of your to-dos or possessions is harmful in itself, but there's a point where one person cannot do it all or take care of it all successfully, least of all happily. Are there things you can delegate, postpone, or get rid of that would free you to truly enjoy what you have?

10

Above all things, revere yourself.
Pythagoras

What a thrill to bask in the praises of others! Yet even hearing their applause pales compared to hearing applause from yourself. Even if no one around you makes you feel good about yourself, feel good about yourself anyway. No matter who you were or who you are now, God can use you to accomplish His good and lasting purpose. Celebrate all God's awesome creation—and that includes *you*.

M A Y

11

Every calling is great when greatly pursued.
Oliver Wendell Holmes

Snow White's dwarves knew the secret to getting a job done—whistle while you work! Now, depending on where you work, your whistling out loud might draw quizzical stares and even a disapproving frown from management. But wherever you go about your daily routine, you can keep a "whistle" in your heart. A happy tune makes any job easier...and puts a happy smile on your face!

12

Anger is a bad counsellor.
Proverb

Whether or not you're a mother, you can lavish the children around you with smiles, warmth, and acceptance. It's important, because every child needs a circle of grownups who cherish them, encourage them, believe in them, and guide them by word and example. They need people both inside and outside the family who will tell them the truth about themselves—that they're unique, loveable and deeply, deeply loved.

M A Y

13

I attribute my success to this:
I never gave or took an excuse.
Florence Nightingale

To encourage means to help build hope, confidence, and courage into the lives of others. Encouragement motivates better than criticism, and initiates change better than accepting excuses. Encouragement speaks truthfully, yet lovingly...firmly, yet with understanding and compassion...practically, yet with respect to the mystery that makes each of us a uniquely created person. Encouraging the best in others brings out the best in you.

14

Forgive us our debts, as we forgive our debtors.
Matthew 6:12

You're a wonderfully gifted and richly blessed woman, but you're also human. That means you will make mistakes—little ones as well as huge ones. Each time, remind yourself that God forgives everyone who comes to Him with a heart of humility and repentance—everyone, and He forgives every confessed transgression. Receive the comfort of His pardon, and then do one more thing—forgive yourself. Next? Stand up and start again!

M A Y

15

Joy is the serious business of Heaven.
C. S. Lewis

Believers in God have every reason to smile! First, they know their heavenly Father, who cares for them. Second, they can lean on His strength in their weakness, and they can ask Him for His wisdom and guidance. Third, they possess the certainty of His presence now and forever. The more they respond to God's love, the more joy they experience and the more joy they give to others. How about your reasons to smile?

16

No time is ever wasted that is spent in wordless solitude.
Author Unknown

Take a break from the TV, radio, computer, and cell phone today. Declare yourself out-of-touch, as if you were standing on a desert island with absolutely no cell tower, satellite, or cable connection. By getting comfortable with silence, you give your thoughts a chance to be heard. By filtering out the voices of others, you allow your own voice to come in. You're likely to hear surprising, wonderful, and marvelous things!

MAY

17

Growing old—it's not nice,
but it's interesting.
August Strindberg

Every age—young, old, and inbetween—has its benefits as well as its challenges. No matter where you are in life, focus on how far you've come...what you know now that you couldn't possibly have known before...the wisdom and experience you have gained as you've grown, dreamed, hoped, discovered, stumbled and gotten right back up again. No one has seen, thought, and done it exactly the same way. You have a story to tell!

18

Keep your friendships in repair.
Ralph Waldo Emerson

Who are the people who encourage you and make you feel good about yourself? Cherish them! When you visit, they leave a song in your heart and a smile on your lips. When you see that special name in your inbox or mailbox, you know you're hearing from someone who truly cares for you and about you. Those whose faces have come to mind right now are your best and truest friends.

19

If I can ease one life the aching...
I shall not live in vain.
Emily Dickinson

It's as easy as opening a door for a mom whose hands are full, or as challenging as using your vacation or holiday time to serve in a soup kitchen feeding the homeless. When you see a need—when someone's difficult situation comes to your attention—consider how you can help. What you feel moved to do may be God's answer to someone's heartfelt prayer.

MAY

20

*Life appears to me too short to be spent
in nursing animosity or registering wrongs.*
Charlotte Brontë

Some women frown because they believe they have
a lot to frown about—a troubled past, a broken
marriage, a difficult circumstance. Who wouldn't
be angry? Yet anger blinds the eyes to the blessings
they possess and shuts the soul to God's readiness
and willingness to comfort, soothe, and strengthen.
Healing takes place in anger-free hearts. Do you
know a woman who needs this kind of freedom?

21

May you live all the days of your life.
Jonathan Swift

Do you hope for a brighter future? Then shine
today. Let the world get a look at your distinctive
beauty and experience first-hand the depth of goodness that continues to grow in your heart. With
God's Spirit at work in you, your words and actions
can't help but glow with the light of His love. A
glimmer of your future is present in the way you
shine your light today.

22

*Not what we have, but what we enjoy,
constitutes our abundance.*
Epicurus

What are ten everyday things that you enjoy doing?
Things you take special pride in (whether anyone
else sees them or not)...things that truly interest
you...things that warm your heart and make you
smile. Make a list! Whenever you feel listless or
bored, unhappy or lonely, take a peek at your list.
There's at least one thing on it that you can do to
chase away the blues!

23

Give us, Lord, a bit of sun, a bit of work,
and a bit of fun.
          Prayer

The balanced life is a life with variety in it. You
need activities that challenge your mind to keep it
sharp, and ones that quiet your mind to keep your
thinking clear and focused. Your body craves movement as much as it requires rest. Your soul, too,
is nourished by the free-flowing thoughts of your
imagination, and the sure words and promises of
Scripture. How can you better balance your life?

24

Life is like playing a violin in public
and learning the instrument as one goes on.
          Samuel Butler

Unlike learning to play the violin, you don't get a
chance to "practice" life before you live it! There are
no rehearsals, backtracks, or re-takes available, yet
learning from past mistakes...growing in wisdom
and insight...and gaining expertise and experience
are there for the taking every day. Let yourself find
pleasure in your "performance"—and remember,
you haven't practiced today, and neither has anyone
else!

MAY

25

All nature wears one universal grin.
    Henry Fielding

If you don't think that God has a sense of humor, consider the duck-billed, beaver-tailed, and otter-skinned platypus! How about the upide-down-looking Baobab tree? But you don't have to visit far-off places to enjoy nature's smiles. Aren't more familiar creations—the parade of animals you can "see" in passing clouds, or the pictures you can "draw" in the nighttime sky—worth a chuckle? Let the Creator hear the sound of your delight!

26

Into each life some rain must fall.
    Henry Wadsworth Longfellow

The sun shines every day, but you don't always see it. Clouds get in the way and obscure its rays. In the same way, daily troubles can gather in your life, and they dim the bright, clear, ever-shining light of God's presence. While you may not be able to part the clouds yourself, God can. Pray that He will open the eyes of your heart to the sunshine of His love.

27

*When you go to bed at night, have for
your pillow three things—love, hope,
and forgiveness. And you will awaken
in the morning with a song in your heart.*
Victor Hugo

When the day is ended, it is ended. No matter what
has happened, let it go. Give thanks for the good
you have received, for the bad you have survived,
and for the progress you have made. Forgive where
forgiveness is called for, and bless those who have
blessed your life. Take no regret, but wisdom alone,
into tomorrow; and then go to sleep with a light
heart, looking forward to a new day of hope, joy,
and fulfillment.

28

*To every thing there is a season,
and a time to every purpose under the heaven.*
Ecclesiastes 3:1

Too bad you can't whip up an extra batch of time to
keep in the freezer for emergencies! Or how about a
few bonus hours once in a while to go out, stay in,
or just relax? Unfortunately, you can't make time;
you have to take it. Always weigh what you're giving
up against what you're getting, and remember to
check the way you're spending your time against
your goals and priorities.

M A Y

29

Whoever said money can't buy happiness didn't know where to shop.

Do you know where to shop for happiness? No, not at that pricey boutique across town (although you might find a darling pair of shoes there), nor even at the gourmet chocolate shop around the corner. "Shopping" for happiness means going to the right places, such as your best friend's place for a chat...your favorite author for a great read...your own backyard to watch the flowers grow. What's on your happiness shopping list?

30

Silences make the real conversations between friends.
Margaret Lee Runbeck

A relationship that's comfortable with quiet has moved beyond expectations and entertainment to genuine devotion. Just being there is enough to know that you're with one of the special people in your life. It's true, too, of your relationship with yourself. Turn off the sound of your own self-talk and bask in the serenity of just being you. Delight in the presence of your closest, dearest friend—you.

31

You are today where your thoughts have brought you; you will be tomorrow where your thoughts take you.
James Allen

Your thoughts matter. They affect your mood, outlook, decisions, actions, and perception of the people around you. The words that come out of your mouth start out as a thought in your mind. Treat your ability to think as the precious gift it is! Let your thoughts consist of heartwarming memories...life-brightening people...inspirational words...strengthening values...God-given purpose... joy-bringing ideas. Anything else is not worth a moment's thought.

A prayer
is the shortest
distance
between
your question
and God's answer.

J U N E

Blessed are they that have not seen,
and yet have believed.
John 20:29

If you could meet God face-to-face for a five-minute Q&A session, what would you ask Him? Perhaps you'd inquire about the accident, illness, or hardship that has had lifelong consequences... the loss of a loved one...the passing of one so young, with so much to live for. You might also wonder why peace is not always possible and why happiness remains elusive for so many.

Actually, there's no taboo question with God. You can ask Him anything in prayer! In fact, He invites you to do so. But then He requests that you listen to His answer—not an unreasonable expectation! You may hear His voice in the depths of a heart overflowing with faith in His care and compassion. You might discover it as you read and study Scripture, listen to counsel of mature Christians, or experience more of the world.

Or you may find He has said, "I'm not going to answer that yet. Wait until the right time. Trust me on this one!" And the most beautiful thing about His answer is that you can trust Him—completely.

J U N E

1

Raise your hand!

If you were shy as a girl, you probably hesitated to raise your hand in the classroom. Perhaps you dreaded the titters of other students if they deemed your question silly, or you were afraid to admit you didn't know the answer already. Don't let those old fears stop you from asking questions today! Your questions, especially those concerning God's plans for your life, show that you're open to learning something new, amazing, and beautiful about God.

2

There is no life that calls for so much
courage and faith as that which seeks
to be led according to the will of God.
    Henry Thomas Hamblin

Though you make practical plans and set realistic goals, you no doubt know that not all things work out the way you want. Sometimes an unexpected event completely derails you, and at other times, you get something much better than you ever could have imagined. "Much better" isn't difficult to accept, for sure! But remember that setbacks often are a blessing in disguise. Watch in faith as God's will unfolds for you.

3

When I saw something that needed doing,
I did it.
    Nellie Cashman

If you wonder what God's will is for you, look around. Most often, His answer lies not in a distant place, but right where you're standing. You probably won't be required to give up all your goods and possessions to follow Him this day, but only to help a child learn a task...call a lonely friend...show a stranger kindness...take on your work with joy and gratitude. Look around, and discover His good will for you!

JUNE

4

*The great pleasure in life is doing
what people say you cannot do.*
Walter Bagehot

If you want to say, "I told you I could!" in the
most convincing way, don't use words. Instead, use
actions. Gather the resources you need, and put
yourself in touch with people who will encourage
and support you as you take practical, observable
steps to reach your objective. Talk about what you
are doing now, and put your future in God's good
and capable hands.

5

Pain is no longer pain when it is past.
Margaret J. Preston

Set your memory on rerun. Recall a time when you
felt as if your life had turned upside down—the time
you threw your hands in the air and cried, "What
went wrong?" Now fast-forward to today. That
event, difficult at the time, was a defining moment
in your life. It has given you the wisdom, experience, and understanding you possess now. Leave
the pain in the past, and celebrate how far you
have come.

6

*Push will get a person almost anywhere—
except through a door marked Pull.*
Author Unknown

If it feels as if you're constantly swimming against
the current, take a little time out to think about
your situation. How do you know that you are not
pitting your own will against God's will for you; or
that you are truly following His path despite the
difficulty involved? It's a good question to ask! Let
His Spirit speak in the words of Scripture, in your
God-given intuition, and in the advice of believing
friends.

J U N E

7

*If I treat you as though you are what
you are capable of becoming,
I help you become that.*
Johann Wolfgang von Goethe

Part of growing up is learning from parents, teachers, and other adults—those who are wiser and more
experienced than yourself. The same thing goes for
spiritual growth, which is a lifelong journey. Keep
going forward spiritually by seeking out mature
Christian women you admire. Ask them how they
meet life's challenges and follow God's will in their
day-to-day routine. And then listen carefully. Allow
them to influence you in wonderful ways.

8

Be not water, taking the tint of all colors.
Proverb

Acceptance...protection...insecurity...intimidation...
habit...women choose to go along with what others
tell them to do for many reasons. While that makes
things comfortable for them, it leaves you stressed,
dissatisfied, and understandably angry. First in
small ways, then in bigger ways, become the distinctive, confident, and beautiful woman God created
you to be. It all starts on the inside—believe, and
then the words and actions will follow.

JUNE

9

We cannot fail in following nature.
Michel de Montaigne

Nature reflects God's perfect timing. Each season has its own work to accomplish, its own challenges, and its own loveliness. The same is true in life. There are things you cannot hurry, no matter how desperately you may yearn for them, and there are hurdles you cannot avoid, no matter how dreaded they are. As you embrace this season of your life, embrace also God's strength, His presence, and His power—because He is embracing you.

10

I am not afraid of storms,
for I am learning how to sail my ship.
Louisa May Alcott

Trying to explain by making excuses rarely fools anyone—and it robs you of an opportunity to learn, grow, and overcome. When things go wrong because of something you have said or done, own up to it. Apologize, make amends where you can, and then move on, wiser and stronger. That way you'll know even better how to navigate through life, and serve as an example to others who find themselves tempted to hide behind an excuse.

JUNE

11

*My only sketch, profile, of Heaven is
a large blue sky, and larger than the
biggest I have seen in June—and in it
are my friends—every one of them.*
Emily Dickinson

Your circle of friends is one of God's many blessings to you. The love and caring, help and support,
encouragement and understanding of friends enrich
your life in a way nothing else can. Give thanks
for your friends and cherish them, all the while
remembering that they reflect the beauty found in
your own heart. It's your gifts of love, kindness, and
insight that God has used to draw them into your
life.

12

Where were you when I laid the earth's foundation?
Job 38:4 NIV

There's no shortage of theories on the beginnings
of the universe, but God—the only one present at its
inception—is the one who knows. In Scripture, He
says that He created it, including every living thing
(including you!) alive on Earth. Further details He
leaves a mystery, perhaps to focus your attention on
something far more important—your willingness to
trust His wisdom, follow His guidance, and believe
He knows the way.

JUNE

13

It's not how old you are,
but how you are old.
Marie Dressler

As you grow older and experience more of life, your
confidence builds and your ability to handle challenges increases. You may find yourself losing some
of the old fears and inhibitions that held you back
in the past, and seeing more of the real you coming
forward. That's why the good habits you put in
place now will serve you well later on. Nurturing
kind, generous, and compassionate ways today is
the best beauty treatment for tomorrow.

14

Look within.
Within is the fountain of good.
Marcus Aurelius

Physical, emotional, or spiritual pain has a purpose.
It lets you know that something's wrong and needs
your attention. Listen carefully! You might need
nothing more than a few hours of rest, or your pain
could indicate something far more serious—something, if caught early, that is easily curable. When in
pain, don't ignore it or medicate it before you investigate it—and give thanks to God for the warning.

JUNE

15

*When we cannot find contentment in ourselves,
it is useless to seek it elsewhere.*
François de La Rochefoucauld

Discontentment is like a race with no finish line. As
soon as you get what you're after, then something
else looms in front of you to take its place. And not
one possession brings the happiness and peace of
mind it promises! Choose to enjoy what you have
right now instead of longing for the next big thing.
"Just a little more" is never enough.

16

*A thankful heart is not only the greatest virtue,
but the parent of all other virtues.*
Cicero

God made both men and women, each with their
own strengths and weaknesses, powers and diffi-
culties, abilities and needs. They were meant to
complement each other, enriching the life of the
other through mutual caring, helpfulness, respect,
and encouragement. Thank God for all the men
who enhance your life—family, friends, coworkers,
associates—and praise the ways they have added and
continue to add to your joy.

JUNE

17

*The best way to cheer yourself up is to
try to cheer somebody else up.*
Mark Twain

A good way to get out of the doldrums is to act like
you're happy. Put on a smile, even if you don't feel
like smiling, and walk with a bounce in your step—
watch others respond to you with a smile of their
own. Think of someone you know who needs cheer-
ing up, and do something to brighten his or her day.
In no time, you'll have forgotten all about the blues,
and life will look (and feel) rosy again!

18

*Be like a postage stamp—
stick to one thing until you get there.*
Josh Billings

Sometimes the toughest jobs are the most worthwhile. Take parenting, for instance. Or how about
working to overcome an addiction, master a com-
plicated skill, or finish a long and difficult project?
Just because something is hard doesn't mean it can't
or shouldn't be done. In fact, it might be the most
worthwhile thing you can do for yourself and for
others! Commitment, patience, stick-to-itiveness—
and a prayer for God's strength and guidance—are
your keys to success.

JUNE

19

No great deed is done by falterers
who ask for certainty.
George Eliot

Before any venture, you'll want to do your home-work—weigh pros and cons, gather your resources, and learn what you can by asking the right questions. Yet there comes a point where you just have to take the leap. No matter how much more preliminary work you put into it, you will never reach absolute certainty that things will go as planned. The only certainty is this: if you don't try, you'll never know.

20

A little fish in a big pond
has a lot of room to grow.

If you're the low woman on the totem pole, look up. Learn everything you can from those above you. Study the characteristics—both personal and professional—that most reflect the woman you aspire to be. All the while, keep in mind how your work is integral to overall success. Doing small jobs with the same excellence you do big jobs is what makes you a leader at any level (and gets you noticed by those ahead of you)!

JUNE

21

We are rich only through what we give.
Anne-Sophie Swetchine

God has a way of turning human reason upside down! People imagine that being rich, important, and successful is all about *getting*. But in God's eyes, the opposite is true. To Him, your wealth, influence, and fulfillment rests in what you are willing to give of your time, talents, resources, and most of all, yourself. Ask God how you can become a truly rich woman by doing things His way—and then do it.

22

Bad times have a scientific value.
These are occasions a good learner would not miss.
Ralph Waldo Emerson

Troubles have a lot to teach—it's learning the hard way, for sure, but if you're paying attention, there's no forgetting the lessons! Adversity forces you to cope with difficult things, but who knows what value your insight and experience will have down the road? At the very least, you'll be better able to empathize with others in the same or similar situation...at best, they will have you to thank for leading them through it.

J U N E

23

Without a purpose, nothing should be done.
Marcus Aurelius

When you learn something new, make it stick! Act on the knowledge you have attained. Put inspiring or motivating concepts into practice in real and tangible ways. What use is it if you simply tuck wisdom away in your mind and it has no good effect on your life? Do it, talk about it, and teach it to others. The more you bring it to mind, the more easily you will be able to make it your own.

24

*Self-knowledge is the beginning
of self-improvement.*
Proverb

Sometimes the most significant personal life questions are those never asked. Why? Fear can play a part—what if that little lump is cancer? What if it's true that...? Yet without bringing these questions out in the open and getting answers from people qualified to help, they'll remain the dark, niggling thoughts that keep you up at night. If there's a question you've been afraid to ask, ask it now. It could make a lifetime of difference.

J U N E

25

Never put off until tomorrow what
you can do today, because if you enjoy
it today, you can do it again tomorrow.
Author Unknown

Once I get a promotion...when the kids are grown...
after I retire... It's often necessary, and smart, to
save until later what doesn't help pay the bills now.
But never put your enjoyment of life "on hold"
until a future time. Even if you can't afford a larger
house, go on a cruise, or devote yourself to vol-
unteering at this moment, embrace today to the
fullest. Be present, attentive, and active now. Love
life as you live it!

26

Change is the watchword of progression.
Ella Wheeler Wilcox

Know when to put sacred cows out to pasture.
What has worked wonderfully in the past can get
woefully out of sync with present needs, trends, and
aspirations. When what you're doing just doesn't
seem to be working quite the way it used to, shake
things up a bit. Ask questions, find out more, be
willing to hear the truth. Make certain the way
you're doing things is still the best way for them to
be done.

J U N E

27

It is the heart always that sees
before the head can see.
  Thomas Carlyle

When you opt to "sleep on it" before making a decision, you're doing a wise thing. That's because while you're sleeping, your brain is at work sorting thoughts, images, and imaginings of the day. Something important you had barely noticed may come to the forefront, and a significant detail you didn't see at first may make all the difference in how you decide to act. "Sleep on it," and let your brain catch up to your heart!

28

A friend is never known until
a woman has a need.

Want to help but not sure where to begin? Start by paying close attention. Family members, friends, acquaintances, fellow church members, and strangers alike are full of clues—both visual and verbal—as to how they're really doing. Pray for the ability to ask the right questions, to understand answers, to discern the underlying feelings and emotions, and to see where you can help. You can be the friend everyone prays to have.

JUNE

29

*Let us be grateful to people who make
us happy; they are the charming gardeners
who make our souls blossom.*
Marcel Proust

Whenever you get the blues, pull out cards and
thank-you notes you've saved. Haven't ever saved
them? Start now, because you probably have more
than you think! They're the best antidote for criticism coming from within or without, and the truest
answers to your questions about your relationship
with others. Read, and re-read, what those who love
you have to say about you. Take this truth to heart.

30

*Go confidently in the direction of your dreams.
Live the life you have imagined.*
Henry David Thoreau

What you wish for might be something that's well
within your grasp. If you think it isn't, ask yourself
why not...discern a real barrier (your loving and
all-knowing God's "no" or "later") from personal
fear or trepidation. If not everything, perhaps some
elements are open to you...if not the whole pie,
maybe a sweet and satisfying slice of it. You will
never know the answer until you ask.

When DOUBT knocks at the door, let FAITH answer.

JULY

Lord, I believe;
help thou mine unbelief.
Mark 9:24

It's hard to hold on to faith when bad things happen. In fact, anything can trigger doubt—anything that raises questions concerning God's presence, His power, His compassion, and His good and gracious will for all people. Think of the times you have lifted your hands and heart to heaven and cried out, "Are you really there, God?"

Yet when you bring your doubts to God, He can use them to increase and strengthen your faith. Though He may not provide a sudden awakening of ardent belief and crystal-clear understanding, He promises to send His Spirit into your heart. It's the Spirit's work to nurture lasting faith, a faith that's healthy, vibrant, alive, firm, and deeply rooted. He will do it.

Just as sunshine warms the summer months, allow the light of God's great love for you to warm your heart and renew your soul. Bring your doubts out into the open and let God's Spirit use them to grow within you the joy of a lively faith in Him.

J U L Y

1

By doubting we come to truth..
Cicero

If you doubt something—whether it's a matter of faith or the truthfulness of what you've heard or read—search for the facts. Doubt works for you instead of against you when it motivates you to seek reliable sources and ask probing questions. When the subject is your relationship with God, look to the Bible, for it's in Scripture that He has revealed what you need to know for a strong, life-giving faith in Him.

2

Why not seize pleasure at once?
How often is happiness destroyed
by preparation, foolish preparation!
Jane Austen

Sometimes the best of times just happen—no one planned, plotted, or strategized beforehand. A chance meeting with a friend develops into a long, leisurely chat over cups of coffee...a last-minute decision to go away for the weekend turns in to one of the most memorable getaways you have ever had. When something good comes your way, don't be afraid to grab it. Let yourself be surprised by serendipity.

J U L Y

3

Everything you do is a self-portrait.

Every task you tackle, word you speak, action you take, and talent you share paints a picture of who you are. Your good attitude, enthusiasm, and willingness to help others add details that will not be missed by those who know you. And when you frame it all with love and joy, you have a masterpiece of art! Let the true you shine through in all you do by autographing your work with excellence.

4

The truth shall make you free.
John 8:32

Freedom to worship according to your beliefs is a great blessing, but you possess an even more important freedom—that's the freedom God gives you through His Son, Jesus. Jesus came to Earth so you could know what God is like, and to make it possible for you to enjoy a strong, loving, and life-giving relationship with Him. Free yourself from uncertainty by delving deeper into the life of Jesus and His work on your behalf.

J U L Y

5

Seek not that the things which happen should happen as you wish; but wish the things which happen to be as they are, and you will have a tranquil flow of life.
                    Epictetus

If you're evaluating a restaurant, movie, or concert performance, you might mention whether or not it met your expectations. But when it comes to your life's circumstances, put away the evaluation form! Instead, open your arms in acceptance—the bad stuff and the blessings alike. Say "yes" to whatever God has permitted to stand in your path, because then you will meet it and use it, and in so doing, find lasting happiness.

6

To love others,
we must first learn to love ourselves.
                    Proverb

Within you, there's a strong, likable woman who has a place in the world—respect her and love her. Decide to build yourself up with sincere compliments, like the ones you'd say to someone you care about. Congratulate yourself when you do well, take a step in the right direction, and overcome (at least for today) a personal challenge. One step at a time will do it—and you can do it!

July

7

If you miss the first buttonhole,
you will not succeed in buttoning up your coat.
Johann Wolfgang von Goethe

They say the first step is the hardest, and it's true. Fears, self-doubt, and sometimes plain old procrastination can keep you from starting a project that you keep saying you plan to do...confronting a situation that isn't going away, no matter how long you ignore it...grabbing hold of an opportunity that holds great promise for you. Go ahead and take the first step. You may be surprised to find how easy the next one comes!

8

If you can't feed a hundred people,
then just feed one.
Mother Teresa

God may not be asking you to take on the world, but He does invite you to take on your corner of it. You have the privilege of touching lives with warmth, friendliness, and willingness to listen. You see things that need fixing, and you can help fix them by sharing your time, abilities, and resources. Wherever you are right now, you can make a God-given difference. So what are you going to do?

J U L Y

9

God gives burdens, but also shoulders.
      Proverb

Burdens come in all shapes and sizes: physical, emotional, and sometimes invisible to all but the person carrying it. Whatever your burden, believe that God has given you whatever you need to bear it—because He has. Within you, there's a well of wisdom and resolve that not only will carry you through, but leave you stronger, more vibrant, and more self-confident. And remember your heavenly Father, whose shoulders are there for you to lean on—always!

10

You risk just as much in being credulous as in being suspicious.
      Denis Diderot

There's no one-size-fits-all response to life events. Some situations warrant caution and suspicion, while others are worthy of your acceptance just as they are. Discernment is key! Your willingness to think through what you see and hear before you react hones judgment, broadens experience, boosts insight, and builds wisdom. Discernment increases the likelihood that you'll shun bogus ideas, and put your faith and trust in the truth.

J U L Y

11

Without risk, faith is an impossibility.
Søren Kierkegaard

It's impossible to follow God without taking risks!
You turn from the seeming certainty of human
reason and open yourself to the mystery of God's
infinite wisdom. You pull away from acceptance
by the world and embrace the possibility of perse-
cution and loneliness. You shun selfish desires and
surrender yourself to God's plans for you. Is faith a
risk worth taking? It's the most important question
you will ever ask yourself.

12

It's easy to say, "Keep your priorities straight."

Balancing what's important with what's urgent
gets tricky at times. Prioritizing equally worthy
goals and activities often calls for tough-minded and
difficult decisions. Choosing whom to answer first
when many need your help and your love is heart
wrenching, at best. Today, bring all your responsibilities to God, and lay them out in front of Him. Ask
Him about His priorities, and then make them your
own with God-given conviction and confidence.

J U L Y

13

Try the ice before you venture on it.
Author Unknown

Doubt puts the brakes on action. It stems from fear of taking the next step, or the memory of hard experience saying, "Caution—you've been this way before!" It sounds like lack of will and confidence talking, or the voice of intuition whispering, "Stop and think before you go any further." Listen to your doubts, but learn to dismiss those that will keep you back and embrace those that will push you forward in the right direction.

14

Those who would be constant in happiness must often change.
Proverb

Ruts may feel like comfortable places to stay, but life changes. While change can bring hardship, it's also the source of newness, discovery, excitement, and growth. Change opens opportunities not possible in the past and discoveries not ready to be made until now. How you treat change determines how change treats you. Greet it with faith, hope, and courage, and you'll find that change is good for you, and good to you!

J U L Y

15

*Those who bring sunshine to the lives
of others cannot keep it from themselves.*
James M. Barrie

The best you can ever give those you love is the
gift of your love. Remove any doubt that you care
for and about them not just with words, but with
actions—those little gestures that mean so much...
the notes that show you appreciate what they do
for you...the time you spend with your attention
focused on them. Giving love away never leaves you
with less, but expands your heart so it can hold
even more.

16

Danger and delight grow on one stalk.
Proverb

Those who get the most joy out of life are those
who put the most risk into it. Though they might
never risk parachuting out of an airplane, they
might risk a cold stare by opening a conversation
with a stranger...embarrassment by stumbling on
the dance floor...criticism by daring to do what
they've always dreamed of doing. Yes, there's danger
out there! But also fun and happiness, joy and
delight. Risk it!

JULY

17

Sow good services;
sweet remembrances will grow from them.
Madame de Staël

During the Renaissance—an era of learning and discovery during the latter part of the fourteenth century through the beginning of the seventeenth century—sculptors made certain their art was as perfect in back as in front, even though the back of the piece often remained largely unseen. The attention you pay to details others may not see or notice says a lot about you. You'll handle what's on view for everyone to examine.

18

Faith is a passionate intuition.
William Wordsworth

It's hard—perhaps impossible—to miss the spiritual side of being human. The real question is not whether it's there, but this: What are you going to do about it? Some would deny it, ignore it, or neglect it in favor of following their own whims and desires. The wiser among us cultivate it by seeking God...asking questions...acting on intuition...listening to that still, small voice of love in each heart...in each soul...in yours.

JULY

19

*The worst loneliness is to not be
comfortable with yourself.*
Mark Twain

You don't have to hunt for what you already possess! Though recognition may come from things like where you went to school, degrees you've received, what you do at work, titles you hold, and achievements you have to your credit, real self-worth was yours even before you were born. God made you, and that means you're eternally, irrevocably, and undeniably worth more than you can possibly imagine. Rest comfortably in that truth.

20

A closed mouth catches no flies.
Proverb

When you talk about others, you're saying a lot about you. Whatever faults or shortcomings you unnecessarily point out about them invites hearers to reflect on yours; unkindly slamming another person merely casts an unflattering shadow on you. There's no better way to put you in a positive light than to put others in a positive light. The old saying, "If you can't say anything good, don't say anything" is still excellent advice!

July

21

A kindhearted woman gains honor.
Proverbs 11:16 NIV

Character traits like physical strength and a power-ful presence command respect. By contrast, kind-ness doesn't command at all—rather, it persuades by the things it says and does. Kindness encourages further kindness by example, and invites admiration through acts of everyday thoughtfulness and con-sideration. When you embrace the best in yourself and in others, you provide an atmosphere of growth and goodness wherever you go. Respect is the natural outcome for all.

22

*We have too many high-sounding words
and too few actions that correspond with them.*
Abigail Adams

Few people of goodwill would argue that honesty, integrity, and truthfulness aren't excellent qualities to have. Possessing them, however, takes more than admiring them or even promoting them. The only way to have excellent qualities is to live them every day in all you do—big and small, public and private. And then you'll never have to tell people how hon-est, reliable, and truthful you are, because the way you act removes all doubt.

JULY

23

There is nothing to make you like other human beings so much as doing things for them.
Zora Neale Hurston

On the sidelines is a good place to be. From there you can help, support, and encourage others on their way to rave reviews. Your applause builds them up, and your continued belief in them gives them what they need to stand again after a stumble. What you do for them increases your understanding, knowledge, and wisdom—and those are important gifts to take with you when it's your turn in the limelight!

24

You are as young as your faith, as old as your doubt... as young as your self-confidence, as old as your fear... as young as your hope, as old as your despair.
Samuel Ullman

It's easy to let numbers rule, especially the number of candles on your birthday cake. But your numerical age doesn't have to dictate what you can or can't do, and you don't want it to. If you're young, you can seek—and possess—wisdom, strength, and confidence. If you're middle-aged and beyond, you can be vibrant, active, optimistic, and inquisitive. Numbers don't count when it comes to the woman you really are!

JULY

25

Hold a true friend with both hands.
Proverb

True friends are precious gifts, enhancing life in a way that nothing else can. Old friends reminisce with you what it was like (or kinda was like) "back in the day"...new friends bring to you their stories, experiences, perspectives, and interests. Friends are the people who are walking beside you and sharing the times of your life with you. Hold them close in your heart...treat them with special care...pray for them often...and let them know how much they mean to you.

26

Everyone should keep a mental wastepaper basket and the older he grows, the more things will he promptly consign to it.
Samuel Butler

In a significant way, your past experiences have shaped you into the person you are today—the opinions, hopes, and dreams you hold are, in large part, a response to what has happened to you and how you perceive it. Accept yesterday, because it's part of your story...but don't let it determine tomorrow. Let go of old thoughts and habits that no longer fit who you want to be...discard what's not working, because you just don't need it anymore.

JULY

27

We only do well the things we like doing.
Colette

To follow your bliss, you first have to find it!
Though there's plenty you *need* to do, take time to
ask yourself what you *want* to do. When you were
a child—before "necessity" took over your life—you
had pastimes. What fascinated you? What activity
did you take to, with no prompting from others?
There are clues, also, in what catches your eye and
piques your interest today. Even if only in a small
way, follow your bliss!

28

Believe not every spirit,
but try the spirits whether they are of God.
1 John 4:1

Have you ever considered how much courage it
takes to express well-founded doubts, ask probing
questions, and not go away until you get meaningful answers? Yes, only the brave take on those in
authority or challenge generally accepted opinions!
But you need even more spunk to examine your beliefs—the comfortable, convenient, and easy-to-un-
derstand ones. Pray for the willingness—and the
courage—to question yourself.

J U L Y

29

My heart is like a singing bird.
Christina Rossetti

When your life is filled to the brim with to-dos and must-dos, you might forget that it's summertime! Set aside at least a few hours (if not a few days) to revel in the sunshine. Relive one of those lazy, "boring" days of long ago, when the time between end-of-school and beginning-of-school seemed to stretch forever. Take a vacation in your own backyard—sometimes that's the best kind of all.

30

Resolve to be thyself.
Matthew Arnold

If there are things about you that you're not proud of, find what you can do to become more like the person you want to be. Accept only genuine change, the kind that starts on the inside and works its way out in the things you say and do. Why? Because anytime you act like someone you're not, fear of being found out will undermine you. Opt for authenticity. Genuine outshines imitation every time.

JULY

31

Wonder is the basis of worship.
Thomas Carlyle

What if today you were to experience life for the
very first time? In some ways, you do. Each day is a
new creation...each question and each answer move
you toward a broader perspective...each encounter
increases knowledge and capability...each moment
of joy and love deepens your understanding of what
life is all about. For a fresh, joy-filled experience,
approach today with simple wonder, curiosity, and
gratitude.

God is
everywhere...
even at
your wits end.

AUGUST

I am with you always,
even unto the end of the world.
Matthew 28:20

"God, are You really there?" The question is an all-too-human cry for some assurance that God remains involved in the life He has created. And His answer? It's a resounding "Yes!"

Though your emotions may not detect His presence or your heart experience the stirrings of His Spirit, He is with you 24/7. But you don't feel it! Perhaps God wishes to strengthen your faith in Him by inviting you to believe even when belief isn't easy. The distance you feel sometimes does not reflect reality, because His promises never fail, and He has promised to be with you always, even to the end of time.

Look at the sun and stars, flowers and trees, rippling ponds and trickling streams—see His world. Listen to His whispers of love in the wind and the waves—hear His voice. Delve into your heart of hearts and reflect on the marvel of your life and breath—know that He is there. Read His words in Scripture, and believe.

AUGUST

1

We cannot go where God is not,
and where God is, all is well.

When are the times you most long for God's
presence? Perhaps it's when you're scared, lonely,
overburdened...or completely at your wit's end!
Take a few minutes' timeout for a couple slow, deep
breaths to help relax your body and mind. Imagine
God standing right beside you, your hand in His,
His eyes on yours. Envision His smile of assurance
and His words of caring. Let your heart embrace
the truth of His presence.

2

We conquer by continuing.
George Matheson

Very often, feelings of frustration stem from daily
routines, responsibilities, or obligations you may
find burdensome. While you continue to do what's
required of you, you'd rather—much rather!—be doing something else. But there are many reasons you
opt to stick with it. What are they? Define them and
say why they're important to you. Replace frustration with faithfulness, and know the fulfillment that
comes with following the right path.

August

3

A change of heart is the essence of all other change and is brought about by re-education of the mind.
Emmeline Pethick-Lawrence

Within families and among friends, a few careless words or one thoughtless action can create an atmosphere shadowed by anger and hard feelings. Sometimes decades pass with both parties waiting for an apology from the other! When rifts or misunderstandings occur, refuse to sweep them under the rug. Make the first move toward honest communication. Get the conversation started by extending love and grace where it's needed most.

4

Beauty is not caused. It is.
Emily Dickinson

Most women want to feel beautiful. Unfortunately far too many look for beauty in all the wrong places! Even if you were to possess the world's most gorgeous hair, face, and figure, you would not feel beautiful unless you believed yourself beautiful. When you look in the mirror today, tell yourself that you are beautiful—because that's the truth. Nothing on the outside can match the loveliness of you when you feel good about yourself.

AUGUST

5

Always be a little kinder than necessary.
James M. Barrie

The best antidote for that down-in-the-dumps feeling is doing something nice for somebody. It's as easy as opening a door for a mom whose hands are full, or as challenging as using your vacation time to help in your local soup kitchen. When you see a need, consider how you can help. Your kind words or actions will not only lift the spirits of another person, but lift your spirits, as well.

6

All life is an experiment.
The more experiments you make, the better.
Ralph Waldo Emerson

Life is full of good, wholesome, God-given opportunities. Each one is an invitation to push yourself beyond the limits of what you think you're able to do. Each is a chance to gain knowledge, explore interests, deepen understanding, and broaden experience. Who knows what you're really capable of until you try what you've never done before? Take one of your "maybe someday" dreams and bring it one step closer to becoming reality.

7

When you feel dog tired at night,
maybe it's because you've growled all day long.

It might start with a cup of spilled coffee or a traffic jam on the expressway that makes you late for work—and then it's downhill all day long! But it doesn't have to be that way. Get into reverse-mode by refusing to let small annoyances become big problems. Keep things in perspective with humor, laughter, patience, and tolerance. A lighthearted shrug and a smile are all it takes to turn a not-so-good beginning into a great ending.

AUGUST

8

Ask, and it shall be given you; seek, and ye shall find; knock, and it shall be opened unto you.
Matthew 7:7

Although God knows what you desire, He invites you to ask Him anyway. The reason? Perhaps to help you clarify your request and point you toward God's answer. Or to remind you that God is the source of all your blessings, and He is the one to thank. Or maybe He just likes to hear the sound of your voice! If there's something you'd like to have in your life, delight God by asking for it.

9

He who undervalues himself is justly undervalued by others.
William Hazlitt

No matter how old you are, where you live, or what you do, there's a negative stereotype that someone could apply to you. Don't listen to them—or to yourself either, if there's a voice inside you that tries to pin an ugly label on you. Replace it with the voice of God, who created you for a purpose and who loves you. Listen to the words of those who appreciate you for the lovely woman you are.

10

The best doctors in the world are Doctor Diet, Doctor Quiet, and Doctor Merryman.
Jonathan Swift

When you aren't feeling your best, even a non-eventful day can get you down. And when the day is chockfull of urgencies and emergencies? You're done for! You can deal with ordinary and not-so-ordinary days more effectively after a good night's sleep, a healthy breakfast, and a few minutes' timeout to focus your mind on your day's tasks and activities. Not only will you feel better during the day, you'll enjoy it more, too!

A U G U S T

11

What we learn with pleasure we never forget.
Louis-Sébastien Mercier

You don't have to enroll in a class to learn something new. If you'd like to know more about gardening or bird calls, the night sky or the weather map, find information in books and on websites— or better yet, join a club and let others teach you. Let your curiosity lead you to the library, special interest groups, and wherever you can explore, discover, and learn more about the world. Become a lifelong student!

12

Where there is patience and humility,
there is neither anger nor vexation.
Francis of Assisi

Genuine humility is life's reality check. It never requires you to put yourself down, nor to allow others to put you down. It only asks you to give both criticism and compliments the same weight...to assess your shortcomings as well as your strengths... to acknowledge the part that others have played in shaping who you are today. Humility never trumpets itself, but gracefully and gratefully receives praise when it comes—and praise will surely come.

AUGUST

13

*Treat your friends as you do your pictures
and place them in their best light.*
Jennie Jerome Churchill

Look for the best in the people around you. Even
the annoying coworker has her positive points
(who knows what she's dealing with at home?), and
the irritating neighbor possesses at least one good
quality (well-hidden, perhaps). When you meet
people, focus on their humanity, their needs, their
strengths. Be generous with compliments—if you
like the color tee-shirt she's wearing, say so. Love
others as you wish to be loved.

14

The past is not a package one can lay away.
Emily Dickinson

You can't go back and change even a second of
your past, but you can control how it affects your
thoughts and attitude today. Banish regret; learn the
lesson your past has taught you, and then leave it in
the past. Cherish the happy moments of your life
and preserve them in your heart. Thank God for the
pleasure and privilege of having them written into
your life's story.

AUGUST

15

Enthusiasm is the greatest asset in the world...
It is nothing more or less than faith in action.
Henry Chester

If you want to become a more interesting person, immerse yourself in interesting things. Your passion for sports, sewing, scrapbooking, photography, cooking, fashion, music, art, movies—whatever makes your heart skip a beat—is your avenue to getting more enjoyment out of life. Pursue your passion—learn about it, keep up with trends, and share your knowledge and enthusiasm. When you're enjoying life, others will enjoy having you around.

16

One kind word can warm three winter nights.
Proverb

Do you know that you have the power to make someone's day? Whether it's a word of encouragement, an impromptu hug, an invitation to your next get-together, or a quick text that reads, "I'm so glad you're my friend," you can lift someone's spirits in less than a minute. Need proof? Remember how you suddenly felt so good inside the last time someone did the same for you!

AUGUST

17

Do not let the sun go down while you are still angry.
Ephesians 4:26 NIV

If you feel your temper flaring, choose to act rather than react. Ask for a few minutes timeout, and then step away from the situation. Use the time to thoughtfully and carefully consider what you're going to do next. No matter who started it or what led to the argument in the first place, respond with words and actions that promote understanding over escalation...grace over getting even...peace over pride.

18

*Everyone makes mistakes—
just don't respond with encores.*

The word "repent" means to turn around—to experience heartfelt sorrow for a personal failing, along with a sincere desire and intention to avoid making the same mistake again. It's the certainty of God's forgiveness and His Spirit at work in you, though, that gives you the power to turn in a new, positive, wholesome, and God-pleasing direction. True repentance brings true forgiveness—you're free to go forward!

AUGUST

19 *Great wealth and contentment
seldom live together.*
Author Unknown

True riches cannot be held in your hand or counted
in dollars. You know that, but do you believe it?
Ask God to see as He sees, and your eyes will be
opened to the treasures of family and friends...the
wealth of faith, hope, and joy...the prosperity of
peace and contentment...the warmth of grace and
gratitude...the beauty of a loving heart. Unlike
material goods, these are the possessions that have
the power to give you everything they promise.

20 *It is hard to fail, but it is worse never
to have tried to succeed.*
Theodore Roosevelt

Not every woman is gifted with perfect pitch, a
green thumb, an artistic flare, or technological
genius. Prodigies and superstars are exceptions, not
the norm. Free yourself from the restricting and
joy-dampening idea that you're in competition with
others, that you have to win first prize, or that you
must shine in everything you do. Not at all. You
don't have to be the best, just do your best—and
most important, enjoy yourself!

AUGUST

21

Remember, Moses started out as a basket case!

Perhaps right now you're standing in a rough place—or you know someone who is. But it's when human eyes can see no way out and human hands can offer no effective help that God's work among us becomes most evident. From miraculous turn-arounds to gradual but lasting healings of body and mind, God brings about His purpose from even the bleakest of circumstances. As long as there is life, there is hope.

22

She who begins many things finishes but few.
Proverb

Starting a new project is fun. You get to plan, gather materials, and enjoy the thought of the finished product. But somewhere along the line, energy wanes and time closes in. A few wrong turns add delay and frustration. Finishing takes dedication and perseverance! That's why it wise to count the cost—time, money, energy—before you begin. And then once you begin, keep moving forward toward completion, even if it's only one small step at a time.

August

23

Friendship is a sheltering tree.
Samuel Taylor Coleridge

Patience...kindness...generosity...forgiveness...you gladly extend these things to those you love, and their love for you brings comfort, fulfillment, and joy to life. But don't neglect the one who's closer to you than anyone else, and that's you. Extend to yourself patience with your rate of progress... kindness in thought and word...generosity in encouragement and affirmation...forgiveness for your shortcomings. Be your own best friend forever.

24

Joy is an elation of spirit—of a spirit which trusts in the goodness and truth of its own possessions.
Seneca

Moments of happiness come and go...good fortune passes and difficult times emerge...moods swing from laughter to sorrow, from elation to disappointment...circumstances shift from ease to hardship, from applause to silence. But joy—that inner well of gratitude for life and delight in whatever blessings surround you—is a constant, lasting, and limitless source of strength. It is a gift of God. Reach out your hands and receive His joy every day.

AUGUST

25

Sympathy is two hearts tugging at one load.
Charles Henry Parkhurst

Grief, discouragement, sorrow, and frustration are burdens meant to be shared. When you are troubled, take your tears to God. Receive His comfort, and ask Him to bring someone into your life who will listen, care, and keep you in thought and prayer. And remember that He may ask you to do the same for someone else. Your presence, your understanding, your touch, and your prayers can lighten the load of another.

26

I expect to pass through life but once.
If, therefore, there be any kindness I can show,
or any good thing I can do to any fellow being,
let me do it now, for I shall not pass this way again.
William Penn

You never know when an opportunity for kindness will dart out right in front of you! Sometimes it can take you so much by surprise that only later do you realize what you could have said or should have done, but didn't. Forgive yourself, and forgive those who may have missed a chance to extend a kindness to you. Ask God to help you remain attentive, willing, and ready to offer kindness whenever and wherever you can.

A U G U S T

27

It is best to do things systematically, since we are only human and disorder is our worst enemy.
Hesoid

The more jam-packed your To-Do list and the more crowded your calendar, the more frantic you feel. You find yourself dashing from place to place and activity to activity—that is, of course, if nothing gets in your way, like a phone call, knock on the door, or several red lights in a row. For your own sanity, schedule yourself some wiggle room. That way, when interruptions come or opportunities arise, you won't slide into panic mode.

28

Always keep your words soft and sweet, because one day you might have to eat them.
Proverb

Not everything that pops into your head needs to be said aloud. If you doubt its appropriateness...if you think it could be taken the wrong way...if you believe it might offend...don't say it. The lasting consequences of ill-spoken words are not worth the momentary pride of delivering a witty line or hearing someone laugh at your comment. What you choose *not* to say can be as much of a gift as what you *do* say.

AUGUST

29

She who makes no mistakes makes nothing.

No one gets it perfect every time, regardless of what "it" is. In fact, if you find yourself making very few mistakes, it could be that you haven't attempted anything new or ventured outside your area of expertise for a long, long time! Release yourself to reach, try, stumble, and maybe even blow it occasionally. Learn from what happened and move on—just avoid making the same mistake more than once!

30

The fruit that can fall without shaking indeed is too mellow for me.
Mary Wortley Montagu

Anything worthwhile having is worth the struggle to reach it. That's true not only for goals like getting a higher education or receiving a position of increased responsibility, but for spiritual goals, as well. If you desire a deeper understanding of Scripture, clearer evidence of your convictions in your words and actions, or a closer walk with God, you may face struggle. Yet it's this very struggle that strengthens you to the point where you can succeed!

31

Peace of mind is an inside job.

You can possess peace of mind even in stormy circumstances. Lean on God whenever the winds get rough—let Him be your sure and steady anchor. Delve into that quiet place in your heart where you can refresh your thoughts and renew your energy. Let God's Spirit strengthen the faith, hope, and love within you so you can do whatever you can to calm the storm, even if all you can do right now is pray.

Don't worry
don't fret...
God will work
things
out yet.

S E P T E M B E R

We know that all things work together
for good to them that love God.
Romans 8:28

Even the most well thought out plans can go awry. Unforeseen circumstances, actions of others, and your own change-of-mind can find you in a place—physical, spiritual, or mental—that you never could have imagined. Now what?

For many, this is when worry takes over. Nights spent tossing and turning, mulling through scary scenarios of what could lie ahead...days taken up with fanciful strategies intended to get you back on track. But there's also another way, a way that calls for faith in God's promises and reliance on His wisdom—it's called trust. Trust that God can and will work things out to your benefit. Trust that God knows the path ahead much better than you do, and it's safe to leave it in His hands.

Are you worried about your circumstances? The circumstances of someone you love? Give your worries over to God in prayer, wait on Him, and He will show you what to do, what to say, in His good time. Easy? No. It's hard—but it's the surest way to deeper faith, discernible courage, and a fret-free mind and heart.

SEPTEMBER

1

Worry sprinkles salt in the wound
and sand in your mental machinery.
    Fred D. Van Amburgh

Have you ever been so worried that you couldn't think straight? It's true, you couldn't, because worry clogs the mind with so much fear, doubt, and anxiety that logical reasoning becomes nearly impossible. Sensible, fact-based decisions slip beyond reach when worry takes over. Turning off the worry-meter is essential if you're facing worrying times, because that's exactly when you want the ability to think, speak, and act carefully, thoughtfully, and wisely.

2

We must reserve a little back-shop, all our own,
entirely free, wherein to establish our true liberty
and principle retreat and solitude.
    Michel Montaigne

Every day, declare a few minutes' mental and emotional timeout. Banish concerns, problems, and pressing issues (without a doubt they'll still be there five minutes later), and treat yourself to a soothing cup of tea...immerse yourself in music you love...take in the calming fragrance of flowers...indulge in a quiet, simple pastime that brings you pleasure. When you're ready to return to the "real world," you'll likely bring a whole new outlook with you.

SEPTEMBER

3

Believe there is a great power silently working all things for good, behave yourself and never mind the rest.
Beatrix Potter

Worry tells you that something is wrong. No, it's not chaotic circumstances or frightening news, but something far deeper—something spiritual. Worry moves in wherever there's a gap between your thoughts and trust in God. Worry reveals a heart not reliant on God to bring things around. It wreaks havoc on your mind, because worry puts all the burden of "fixing things" on you when God is saying, "Hey, let Me handle this!"

4

Time is never lost that is devoted to work.
Ralph Waldo Emerson

Are you doing the work—paid or volunteer—that you truly feel you are meant to do? If you can say "yes," give thanks, for you are living your God-given vocation! But if you hesitated to say yes, take heart, because God has a plan and a purpose for you. What you're doing right now is a step toward reaching your potential, perhaps bringing you the strength, experience, knowledge, and know-how that will prove invaluable later on.

S E P T E M B E R

5

There is not much danger that real talent
or goodness will be overlooked long;
even if it is, the consciousness of possessing
and using it well should satisfy one.
Louisa May Alcott

Knowing you've done a good job, performed
superbly, or attained a high level of learning is one
thing. Making sure everyone else knows is quite another! Don't hide your accomplishments, but don't
crow about them either. Though what you say may
be true, boasting serves to put others down while
lifting oneself up. Instead, allow others the pleasure
of tooting your horn. It makes for a more pleasant
melody all around.

6

What you think means more than anything
else in your life.
George Matthew Adams

Are you "for" or "against" yourself? Here's a quick
way to check: Think back on some of the self-talk
you've engaged in lately, and recall how, in your
mind's eye, you often picture yourself. Describe
how you believe others perceive you—chances are,
it's more about how you perceive yourself! You have
enough challenges in this life without the burden
of a rocky relationship with yourself. Deal compas-
sionately with everyone, including you.

7

*A wise woman cares not
for what she cannot have.*

A lot of frustration stems from striving to get what God has withheld. Whether He says, "No, not now," or "No, not ever," accept His decision. Imagine yourself putting that particular desire in a box, and then gently storing it on a high shelf. Now your arms are free to receive the blessings—the abundant blessings—He has for you right now. Listen for His "Yes," because your real happiness lies there.

8

Best friend, my well-spring in the wilderness!
George Eliot

A best friend is a treasure. She or he is the one you can talk to about anything and not worry that you'll be judged or criticized. When they say, "What can I do to help?" you know there's a genuine willingness and desire to help...when they offer comments or advice, you know the words come from a heart that deeply cares. You can share your joys—and your burdens—with them, because that's what friends are for.

9

*Be always resolute with the present hour.
Every moment is of infinite value.*
Johann Wolfgang von Goethe

Sometimes life can feel as if you're racing at 100 miles an hour! But what if you're going so fast that you're missing blessings and opportunities along the way? Or what if you're headed the wrong direction? Look at your life with a critical eye. Where do you want to be a year from now? Five years? Make sure the road you're on is leading there—and if it is, take time to enjoy the scenery!

SEPTEMBER

10

There's no pillow as soft as a clear conscience.
Proverb

When your conscience talks, listen. Your conscience
serves to heighten your awareness that something is
wrong and increase your sensitivity to those times
you have not said or done the right thing. Its voice
is like a warning siren, and the louder it sounds, the
better! When you hear your conscience speak, do
your part to right a wrong the first chance you get.
You'll sleep, breathe, and smile so much easier.

11

A day of sorrow is longer than a month of joy.
Proverb

It's difficult, if not impossible, to fathom "why"
when tragedy strikes. Yet, in each life, there are
times of profound sorrow, intense anxiety, and un-
answerable questions. Let your heart turn to God's
all-knowing and all-compassionate presence whenever human understanding fails. He can handle tears
and anger...fear and anxiety...disgust and revulsion
and hatred. His Spirit at work in you has the power
to transform your heart and mind, even if you won't
have all the answers.

12

I know the plans I have for you...
plans to prosper you and not to harm you,
plans to give you hope and a future.
Jeremiah 29:11 NIV

Mothers worry about kids long after they're
"kids"—and mother or not, you may worry about
nieces and nephews, friends and relatives, neighbors
and coworkers. You might worry about yourself,
too—what will your future bring? Whatever your
worries and concerns, God's promise holds firm.
Your future and the future of your loved ones rest
in His hands. You have no reason to worry, but
every reason in the world to give thanks.

SEPTEMBER

13

If I have seen further,
it is by standing on the shoulders of giants.
Isaac Newton

What you've accomplished so far would not be possible without those who have gone before you. The physical and emotional support, guidance, training, and education they've offered has put you in a position to build on what you've learned and learn even more. Ideas and inventions of the past are yours to use, explore, and expand for your wellbeing and for the benefit of those around you. Just think—you may be the inspiration that moves future generations!

14

To wish to act like angels while we are
still in this world is nothing but folly.
Teresa of Avila

Being honest and candid about your fears, failures, and imperfections is a sign of confidence. It shows you are self-aware and comfortable in your own skin. You have no need to surround yourself with an air of bravado, but can present yourself to others as you are—a woman loved by God, with particular strengths and particular weaknesses. Your reality-based self-confidence encourages others to express their true feelings and heartfelt thoughts.

SEPTEMBER

15

It is the heart which experiences God,
and not the reason.
Blaise Pascal

Consider the wonder of being human—of possessing life and breath, the ability to move, think, feel, dream, hope, love. And then reflect on the marvels of nature—from tiny organisms to distant stars, from sea's depth to mountain's peak. God's creation points to Him, the Master Artist who cares about what He has made. He cares so much that He sent His Son Jesus to help you know Him better. How well do you know Jesus?

16

Happy is she who conducts herself honorably.
Proverb

What's expedient or convenient isn't necessarily the wrong thing to do—in fact, it can be a welcome time-saver that frees you to focus on something more important. But no matter what the circumstances, speed and ease should never outweigh what's kind, honest, prudent, or truthful. An ill-advised shortcut, once exposed, will undermine your good reputation—and it will be a long time, if ever, for you to regain it.

SEPTEMBER

17

*There is no such thing in anyone's life
as an unimportant day.*
    Alexander Woollcott

Even if it's a routine day, what you think, do, and
say matters. That's because you matter! God would
not have you at this time and in this place without
a purpose. Although it's possible you have every
intention of moving on very soon, right now there's
something you can do to bring meaning and joy to
yourself and others. Today you have an opportunity
to live, learn, and love, so seize it with open arms.

18

*The real voyage of discovery consists not
in seeking new lands, but seeing with new eyes.*
    Marcel Proust

When you're visiting someplace new, you're all eyes!
You want to soak in the sights and take in everything that's around you. Yet familiar places—where
you live, work, shop, and play—hold mystery and
wonder, too. Take time to look—really look—at the
objects in your home, the scenery you pass on your
way to the store, the faces of people in your own
community. Be all eyes wherever you are today, and
see with new eyes.

SEPTEMBER

19

What soap is to the body, laughter is to the soul.
Proverb

A little silliness is good for the soul. Teach yourself to look on the funny side, especially when it comes to what worries you or frustrates you. Take time out to do something playful and frivolous just because you can. Laugh often. Bring out the kid in yourself and in others by generously sharing clean, kindhearted humor—it releases tension, defuses conflict, calms emotions, relieves stress, brightens moods, and brings on smiles.

20

Reality is not a show.

What you see in movies and watch on TV is entertaining, but the depiction of life, love, sex, relationships, and appearance that you get is all make-believe. Some viewers, however, so admire the exciting and glamorous lives they see on-screen that they become discontent with their own seemingly "dull" lives. If you find yourself feeling unhappy with yourself or your life after watching, it's time to find more positive, wholesome, and uplifting shows.

S E P T E M B E R

21

Fear not: for I am with thee.
  Isaiah 43:5

You can't avoid situations of grave concern—circumstances that threaten your health and wellbeing, the safety of your family, or the preservation of a relationship you cherish. But you can avoid sinking into hopelessness. Determine that you will not despair, but entrust your worry and fear to God in a spirit of gratitude for His presence in your life. Free your heart and mind to hear His counsel and discover a positive response to the situation.

22

*Decide on what you think is right,
and stick to it.*
  George Eliot

Second guessing your decisions can leave you frustrated, confused, regretful, and headed nowhere. Trust yourself to make the best decisions you know how, given the information and resources at hand, your intuition at the time, and the guidance you receive from prayerfully considering God's will and purpose. If it happens that you make a poor decision, learn what you can from it and go on; you are stronger and wiser now.

SEPTEMBER

23

The sovereign cure for worry is prayer.
William James

When you get to the point where you've done all you can do, there's still something you can keep on doing—pray. While hand-wringing has no power to change anything, hand-folding does. Prayer puts the burden of finding a solution where it belongs—on God. It relieves your heart and clears your mind so you'll be able to see God's hand in the way things turn out. It frees you to focus on His blessings, His way, His wisdom.

24

Courage is often caused by fear.
Proverb

Who makes you feel inadequate? Think why you react this way around a particular person. Are you afraid of what they might do to you...awestruck by their wealth, fame, power, or authority...intimidated by their education, skill, or personality? Take responsibility for your reaction. Identify why you feel the way you do. Perhaps there's a real reason, but a better way of responding to it; or it's simply a runaway emotion on your part that you can control.

SEPTEMBER

25

God often visits us,
but most of the time we're not at home.
Joseph Roux

When you feel a need to spend a few quiet moments
in prayer...to reflect on something you have seen
or heard...to reach out to someone in love and
compassion...to consider the consequences of what
you're about to do...to give your fears and worries
to God...to remember that you're deeply loved and
cherished...listen. Listen carefully! God may be
making a "heart" call through the voice of His
Spirit living and working in your life.

26

Fame is a fickle food upon a shifting plate.
Emily Dickinson

Friends are more important than fans. There's no
way even hundreds of fans can take the place of one
good friend who will listen to you, care about you,
and stick by you whether you're popular or not.
A long list of social media followers means nothing,
because not one is likely to be there for you when
you need help, support, or encouragement. It isn't
the breadth, but the depth of your relationships
that makes them meaningful.

SEPTEMBER

27

Fear makes the wolf bigger than he is.
Proverb

Worry acts like a magnifying glass. It zooms in on one situation or circumstance and makes it larger-than-life. It prompts wild imaginings of everything that could happen, could get worse, could result in the future because of what's taking place right now. Yes, things could go from bad to worse—but will they? Worry won't tell you; God alone knows. Separate rational concerns from irrational flights of fear before making your next move.

28

Make wisdom your provision for the journey from youth to old age, for it is a more certain support than all other possessions.
Diogenes

When you read or hear words that uplift you, commit them to memory. Jot down sayings and affirmations that are meaningful to you, and put your notes where you will see them every day... delve into—even wrestle with—observations that strike you as deeply true. Keep special pages in your journal for poems, quotations, and verses from the Bible so you can turn to them whenever you feel in need of a mental or spiritual pick-me-up.

September

29

The first hour is the rudder of the day.
Henry Ward Beecher

Contrary to a popular saying, there's no right or wrong side of the bed to wake up on! What matters is how you choose to greet the day. A sure way to get yourself off to a good start? Allow yourself ample time to get ready, enjoy a healthy breakfast, and spend a few minutes with God in prayer. A grateful heart and an optimistic attitude, too, make for a wonderful wake-up call!

30

You can't get what you want until you know what it is.

Fretting, whining, and complaining come easy. Defining exactly what you would like to see take place or do differently, and then devising a realistic way to put your wishes into effect, takes work. First, put dissatisfaction aside and figure out what you're really after. Second, objectively determine whether it's the situation or your attitude—or both—that needs adjustment. Third, do your part to make that happen.

God adores
the sound of
your voice
talk to
Him
often.

OCTOBER

Call to me and I will answer you.
Jeremiah 33:3 NIV

God invites you to pray! That is, He offers you the privilege of speaking with Him about whatever is on your mind. Like someone who loves you (and He loves you deeply), He enjoys hearing the sound of your voice...and listening to your silences when you can't find the words to say.

Of course God already knows your needs, understands your hurts, and can read the desires of your heart, yet He encourages you to tell Him. Prayer reminds you that all good things come from His hand, and that your comfort, strength, and confidence stem from His Spirit at work in you. Your words serve to help you clarify your thoughts and focus your attention on His power, His help, and His will.

Daily prayer puts you in touch with God and with yourself. Even if your prayer-time lasts only a few minutes, it allows you a chance to express your gratitude to God and place your requests before Him. Prayer opens your heart and soul to the help and comfort, the beauty and blessings God has for you every day.

OCTOBER

1

Vision is the art of seeing the invisible.
Jonathan Swift

Those who can look beyond today to what might be tomorrow's reality are said to have vision. With inspiration and imagination, they can "see" possibilities neither visible nor apparent to others. Similarly, prayer opens your spiritual eyes. With your heart and mind attuned to God's work in your life, you begin to see what others cannot. Constant, attentive prayer lets you perceive His will and allows you to more clearly discern His wisdom.

2

Don't be afraid to take a big step if one is indicated. You can't cross a chasm in two small jumps.
David Lloyd George

Perhaps there's a change for the better that you'd like to see take place in your personal situation, job, relationships, financial standing, or spiritual life. If you keep putting it off, it will never happen! There comes a now-or-never time when you've got to take a leap of faith and embark on a plan of practical action. Sure, weigh the risks and get advice and pray. But when your gut says "Leap!" - leap!

OCTOBER

3

Nothing is too small a subject for prayer,
because nothing is too small to be the
subject of God's care.

Henry Thomas Hamblin

When you're completely stressed out over some minor mishap, prayer might be the last thing on your mind! After all, why would God care about the kids' muddy footprints on the kitchen floor, or the loaf of bread you forgot to pick up on your way home? Because He loves you and cares about you, that's why. If it's something big enough to bother you, it's big enough to bring to Him in prayer.

4

Courage is fear that has said its prayers.

Dorothy Bernard

You might know what should be done and needs to be done, but you're afraid to do it. Perhaps you fear the fallout of confrontation, intervention, or a difficult conversation. Maybe you wonder about the consequences of approaching your boss, neighbor, parent, or best friend with words you know they don't want to hear. Be bold. Be brave. Go, with prayer in your heart and on your lips. Do what you know needs to be done.

O C T O B E R

5

Friendship doubles our joys
and divides our griefs.
            Proverb

There are times when God's answer to your prayer
is the presence of a friend—someone who is always
there for you. Whether through a look or a touch,
sound advice or comforting words, they show that
they understand and care. You share freely, because
they know what to do with both good news and
bad news, with both celebrations and commemora-
tions. Thank God for the friend whose face has just
come to mind.

6

Search thine own heart;
what paineth thee in others, in thyself may be.
            John Greenleaf Whittier

As an adult, you might have found yourself saying
to the kids in your care something you heard when
you were growing up—something you vowed you'd
never say! In all relationships, you're bound to come
up against certain personality quirks that drive you
nuts. Yet it's possible that you do the same thing.
When someone annoys you, consider the possibility
that your annoyance is not with the person, but
with what it reveals about you.

OCTOBER

7

Unto thee, O Lord, do I lift up my soul.
Psalm 25:1

When you lift up to God the concerns of your heart, your burdens feel lighter...the road ahead seems smoother...your thoughts become calmer... your trust in Him grows deeper...your attitude turns more positive and hopeful. That's the power of prayer at work...the change prayer makes in how you respond to worry, fear, stress, disappointment, sorrows, and setbacks...the strength and comfort God brings to you when you give yourself to Him in prayer.

8

Dreams are the touchstones of our character.
Henry David Thoreau

Are your long-prayed-for hopes and dreams worthy of how much space they're taking up in your heart and mind? If God's "no" has been His answer so far, it's not because He can't do what you ask. It could be, however, His way to prompt you to measure your wants against His wisdom. Perhaps He has more to teach you right where you are...most assuredly He has more ways to bless you than you could ever imagine.

OCTOBER

9

Right is right, even if everyone is against it;
and wrong is wrong, even if everyone is for it.
William Penn

A building is said to have integrity when it sits on a firm foundation and is structurally sound. The same is true of people. A life built on the firm foundation of God's commandments cannot be shaken. Character marked by trust in His wisdom and gratitude for His blessings will not crumble. Thoughts, words, and actions immersed in decency, honor, honesty, truthfulness, and kindness regardless of the circumstances are the lasting building blocks of integrity.

10

When at night you cannot sleep,
talk to the Shepherd and stop counting sheep.
Author Unknown

Considering all aspects of a problem and mulling over possible solutions is one thing—tossing and turning all night long is another! The former uses your God-given reason to help you through a challenging situation, while the latter worsens it. Lacking enough shut-eye, you can't think clearly and are more susceptible to fear, panic, and ill-health. The next time sleep eludes you, turn your problems over to God—after all, He doesn't need the rest, and you do.

OCTOBER

11

Beauty you may have with you always,
if you will but plant beauty in your heart.
Fred D. Van Amburgh

Beauty is more than anything you can get out of bottles, jars, and lipstick tubes—and far less expensive! True beauty shines from the inside out. The best and surest beauty regime starts with kindly thoughts, a sunny attitude, and a generous heart. It gathers enthusiasm, gratitude, patience, respect, love, and gentleness and applies each freely and joyfully throughout the day. By nightfall, real beauty never fades, but remains radiant and at peace with God.

12.

In the kingdom of hope, there is no winter.
Proverb

Perhaps there's someone who has been unkind to you or cheated you. There might be someone whose negative attitude or grating criticisms put you on edge. You may not be able to completely avoid these people, but you don't have to draw close to them, either. And you can do this: Forgive them. Pray for God's best in their lives. Whether or not they ever change, your heart will—and so will the way you look at them.

OCTOBER

13

*In prayer, it is better to have a heart
without words than words without a heart.*
John Bunyan

Sometimes you may want to pray, but the right
words just won't come out. You search the depths
of a heart overflowing with feelings and emotions
that you long to express, yet you can't. This too
is prayer. Take God to the place where you hurt...
where you're mourning...where you're so in need
of the comfort of His presence. Like a good friend,
God doesn't need your words, because He understands your silences.

14

One "no" averts seventy evils.
Proverb

Leading a healthy, happy life means making wise
choices. For a healthy diet, you eat balanced meals
and avoid filling up on junk food. For a healthy
spiritual diet, you read, pray, and meditate on God's
words as you find them in scripture. You avoid
filling up your mind and thoughts with half-truths
and untruths, and sweet-sounding but unscriptural
promises. There are times when the wisest thing to
do is say "no."

OCTOBER

15 *People only see what they are prepared to see.*
Ralph Waldo Emerson

If you look for the best in yourself, you'll find it.
Instead of criticizing yourself, you'll focus on the
times you have spoken kindly, given generously,
acted graciously, and stepped forward confidently.
Give yourself a pat on the back, and your praise will
encourage more "best" behavior. The same is true if
you look for the best in others—you're sure to find
it, and when you do, your compliments will keep
it coming!

16 *Faith is the daring of the soul
to go farther than it can see.*
William Newton Clarke

Sometimes life feels as if you're driving down a dark
road with no headlights. You have no idea what lies
directly in front of you. In truth, even if your days
are precisely planned, you don't know what's up
next. That's why God invites you to put your faith
in Him rather than rely on yourself—He knows
the road, sees what's ahead, and remains in complete control. With Him, you can move forward in
confidence.

OCTOBER

17

Without enthusiasm, every task is difficult.

A lack of options isn't what leaves you feeling lackluster, but lack of inspiration is. Perk up your enthusiasm by shaking up your routine. Try a new route on your way home from work or appointments...pick a library book from a section you haven't yet explored...learn a game or sport you've never played before...discover interesting facts about the place where you live. In a world this big, there's always something new to do or pursue.

18

In the day of my trouble I will call upon thee.
Psalm 86:7

You've heard it said, "As a last resort, read the instructions." Many people use prayer that way, too—as a last resort when everything that can go wrong has gone wrong. Certainly, if you find yourself with no place else to turn, turn to prayer! But why wait? At the first sign of trouble, pray for God's strength, guidance, and reassurance. And when things are going right, pray a prayer of gratitude and appreciation.

19

There is not in the world a kind of life more sweet and delightful than that of a continual conversation with God.
Brother Lawrence

You can talk to God anytime you want to. You don't have to drop what you're doing, or pull over to the side of the road, or find a secluded corner to voice appreciation for His love and care...ask His help in facing a sticky situation or His wisdom to guide you in making a difficult decision...invite His Spirit to deepen your faith and trust... express your gratitude for His many blessings in your life.

20

Love changes the face in the crowd.

Every friend you have today started out as a stranger—someone whose name you didn't know and whose voice you may have never heard before. If you feel shy or self-conscious when you're the newbie of the group, picture everyone around you as someone you already know and love. The more comfortable you feel and more confident you appear, the easier it is to turn today's strangers into tomorrow's friends.

21

To be seventy years young is sometimes far more cheerful and hopeful than to be forty years old.
Oliver Wendell Holmes

No matter how old you are, put your youth to good use. Why waste a minute bemoaning what you can't do when there's so much you can do? Highlight the talents, skills, know-how, and abilities you have today...revel in the wisdom, experience, and maturity you possess now...find joy in the life and breath that is yours at this moment. Feel good about yourself, because you have been through much and you have made it!

22

Money is a good servant but a bad master.
Proverb

Money prompts prayer! The struggle to make ends meet, handle an emergency, and save for the future brings many to their knees. Never hesitate to speak to God about money, because in the Bible, He speaks about it to you. He urges you to spend your money on things that matter and share your money with those in need. No matter how much or how little money you have, God will help you use it well.

OCTOBER

23

*The principal use of prudence, of self-control,
is that it teaches us to be masters of our emotions.*
René Descartes

Feelings are fleeting, and your emotions are not an accurate measure of truth. Certainly, sensations of excitement, passion, love, sorrow, anger, anticipation, joy, and happiness add breadth and depth to life, but giving them power over what you do and say is a mistake. Pay attention to how you feel about things, but balance your emotions with common sense, advice from people you trust, past experience, and a good helping of prayer.

24

When I pray, my heart is in my prayer.
Henry Wadsworth Longfellow

You may have broken places in your life, but you can still be whole. Prayerfully invite God to immerse your soul in the soothing balm of His presence. Let His love mend what misunderstandings, poor choices, and rash words have torn apart. Ask Him to help you accept the scars on your heart, grow in spiritual wisdom, and use your experience to comfort others as He has comforted you. Pray, always pray, for wholeness.

25

Success comes before work only in the dictionary.

The only way to guarantee you'll never fail is to never try. Of course, if you never try, it's guaranteed that you'll never succeed, either. The time, work, and effort it takes to reach your aspirations are well worthwhile. Missteps along the way don't mean you should turn back, but that you've learned something by first-hand experience. And if you don't make it? That's okay, because the real reward is in the journey, and you've made the journey.

26

I like the dreams of the future better than the history of the past.
    Thomas Jefferson

Everyone has a past—successes and failures, accomplishments and regrets. Everyone has the clean slate of today, also. Give yourself and those around you the opportunity to write a different storyline than what's expected. Open a new chapter for yourself by living up to your ideals, acting like your best self, and giving your best effort, even if others are slow to see you in a new light. Keep it up, and the evidence will speak for itself!

27

Prayer is not eloquence, but earnestness.
Hannah More

Do you shy away from praying because you don't know all the words to traditional prayers...you think you don't deserve God's attention...you believe He hasn't time for or interest in your personal hopes and fears, trials and troubles with all the big things going on in the world? Not true! Throughout the Bible, God invites and encourages you to pray. There's no good reason not to pray...and every good reason to do it, and do it every day.

28

Time is what we want most,
but what - alas! - we use worst.
William Penn

When hours and days seem to whiz past you at breakneck speed, it's high time to hit the brakes. Take time out to look at what's around you...appreciate your daily blessings...reconnect with the people who mean the most to you...thank those who have helped you, and continue to help you, become the woman you are today. Even more important, renew your relationship with God. If you're too busy for Him, you're way, way too busy!

OCTOBER

29

Forgiveness is the fragrance that the violet sheds on the heel that has crushed it.
Mark Twain

When you forgive someone, it doesn't mean you're ignoring or excusing the offense. It doesn't mean you weren't hurt, or that it won't take work to fully repair the relationship. Forgiveness means this—you grant full pardon to the person, just as God pardons you. And when you give pardon, you get this—the power to let go of any grudge that could weigh you down or fill your heart with bitterness. Is that a sweet deal, or what!

30

We cannot help conforming ourselves to what we love.
Francis de Sales

Those we admire, we tend to imitate. Do the people you look up to possess traits you would be happy to call your own? Do your friends behave in ways you would feel good about copying? If the answer is "yes," hang out with those people! Hang out with God, too, and immerse yourself in His love and kindness, gentleness and compassion. Let your admiration for Him show in all the things you do to become more like Him.

31

If you do not ask yourself what it is you know, you will go on listening to others and change will not come because you will not hear your own truth.
Saint Bartholomew

Like every person, you have three sides: the person you want people to think you are; the person you think you are; and the person you really are. If any one side hides behind a mask, you forfeit your own distinctiveness. If any facet of your personality wears a costume, you're playing a role instead of being fully yourself. When all three sides of you are identical, that's when you're living as the unique woman God has created you to be.

Take a
little time
everyday to
be thankful.

November

Give thanks unto the Lord.
Psalm 136:1

"Count your blessings!" is something you hear frequently. Especially during this month filled with Thanksgiving celebrations, it's easy to give those words a nod of agreement, and then quickly go on to other, fresher topics.

Like many time-honored phrases, however, "count your blessings" delivers a basic truth. An "attitude of gratitude"—more familiar words!—is the foundation of a joy-filled life. Think of it this way—when someone gives you a wonderful gift or does something special for you, you want to thank the person, and you do so from the heart. Invariably, your "attitude of gratitude" opens you to appreciate the gift and the giver even more.

So what's working in your life? What are the gifts you have right now that you're especially thankful for? What do you like best about yourself, about others, and the world around you? Start counting! The most important part, though is knowing whom to thank—your loving God, the giver of all good things forever.

N O V E M B E R

1

From self alone expect applause.
  Marion L. Burton

When you've given the day your best effort...
accomplished what you set out to do...took an
opportunity to do someone a favor...did or said
exactly the right thing...thank yourself! Maybe
treat yourself to a night in—turn off the cell phone,
power down the computer, and enjoy a bubble
bath...a good book...a favorite movie...a cup of tea.
Give yourself the gift of relaxation in gratitude
for the hard work you've put in today.

2

There is just one life for each of us: our own.
  Euripides

Comparing your body, talents, achievements,
attainments, income, love life, or lifestyle with
anyone else's leads you down one of two roads—
pride or discontent. Pride creates a feeling of
superiority over those you deem less accomplished,
less favored than yourself. Discontent fills your
heart with envy and thanklessness. Neither
direction is pretty! The more you focus on your
own unique journey, the more beauty and
blessings you'll discover along the way.

November

3

*The best place to find a helping hand
is at the end of your own arm.*
Proverb

You never know where the day is going to take you.
Before you hop out of bed, prepare for the best.
Picture yourself feeling good, meeting friendly people, and succeeding in what you plan to do. Bring
to mind at least three people, situations, or things
you're especially thankful for at this particular time,
and express your gratitude to God for His blessings.
Your positive frame of mind will help you, no matter what the day brings!

4

*Apparent failure may hold in its rough shell
the germs of a success that will blossom in time,
and bear fruit throughout eternity.*
Frances Ellen Watkins Harper

Sometimes, when you think you have completely
missed the mark, you haven't. You've simply hit
another mark right on—a mark that's possibly the
one God intended you to hit, even though you
weren't aiming for it. If you're struggling with
failure—a venture gone wrong, a goal attempted
but not reached—take a good look at where you
are now. Failure on one target may well be success
on another.

5

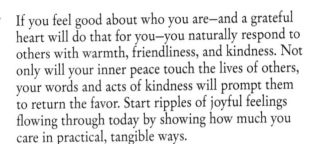

A kind heart is a fountain of gladness,
making everything in its vicinity freshen into smiles.
Washington Irving

If you feel good about who you are—and a grateful heart will do that for you—you naturally respond to others with warmth, friendliness, and kindness. Not only will your inner peace touch the lives of others, your words and acts of kindness will prompt them to return the favor. Start ripples of joyful feelings flowing through today by showing how much you care in practical, tangible ways.

6

In all thy ways acknowledge him,
and he shall direct thy paths.
Proverbs 3:6

For many people, the holiday season is a stressful one. There are meals to plan, relatives to visit, gifts to buy—and all the while, daily tasks, normal activities, and regular duties just keep coming! If you feel holiday stress creeping up on you, take a moment to prayerfully think about what the season means to you, what you would like to see happen, and how you can help others understand the meaning behind the celebrations.

November

7

*Perhaps the most delightful friendships
are those in which there is much agreement,
much disputation, and yet more personal liking.*
George Eliot

A true friend not only accepts, but understands and
embraces, the true you. Yet she can't understand and
embrace what she doesn't know is there. When you're
with a true and trusted friend, risk revealing your
failings, fears, and insecurities, because it's possible
the two of you have more in common than you think.
Share your dreams, and invite your friend's support
and encouragement. The fewer secrets there are
between you, the closer you can become.

8

*The person who has stopped being thankful
has fallen asleep in life.*
Robert Louis Stevenson

Wake yourself up—more than once a day, if necessary! Purposefully give your attention to what
you're doing at the moment, even if it's the most
routine, "boring" task you can imagine. Savor
your food...take in your surroundings...embrace the
awesome experience of possessing life and breath.
Think kindly, speak thoughtfully, give generously,
and live thankfully for all the blessings you enjoy.
Today, reawaken yourself to be fully present in the
present.

NOVEMBER

9

Get to know the stranger inside.

Certain weaknesses only surface when you're stressed, angry, or in pain. When you realize that you haven't been at your best, acknowledge your shortcomings as being part of who you really are. Don't excuse them. Own up to weaknesses and call them what they are, because admission is the first step in controlling them. Habits that put you in a bad light, even if you're the only one looking, are always worth breaking.

10

One day in perfect health is much.
Proverb

If you're feeling good today, give thanks! If you're ill or injured, give thanks, too—thank God for what's working well and the human body's remarkable ability to heal. Give thanks for those who are helping you on the road to recovery, and for those whose presence, comfort, and encouragement mean so much. Whether your health is good or could be better, make the healthiest choice of all—choose gratitude!

NOVEMBER

11

Heroes are revealed, not made.

Service members who show bravery in combat receive medals in recognition of what they have done. But heroic action takes place off the battlefield wherever a challenging, demanding, or dangerous situation is met with strength of character. When you hold on to godly values and principles even when it's inconvenient or may lead to ridicule or discrimination, you're a hero. When you help despite possible harm to yourself, you're a hero. Give thanks for heroes—including you!

12

Far away in the sunshine are my highest aspirations. I may not reach them, but I can look up and see their beauty, believe in them and try to follow where they lead.
Louisa May Alcott

There are seeds of greatness in you. Your abilities, strengths, desires, interests, and dreams all hold marvelous potential. They may lead to discoveries about yourself and about the world that you never could have imagined. No matter where you are in life, cultivate your highest aspirations with enthusiasm, purpose, and perseverance. Enjoy the process of planting and nurturing, and when the season is right, you'll harvest fulfillment and success.

NOVEMBER

13

When I give, I give myself.
Walt Whitman

A good relationship—whether we're talking friend, spouse, coworker, neighbor, or family member—isn't a 50/50 proposition. It's two people giving 110% of themselves to each other. No one keeps score, holds grudges, harbors bitterness, or attempts to assume superiority...but both allow the other to grow, contribute, relax, and be the person they were meant to be. How about you? In your relationships, don't hold back what's within your power to give.

14

Start by doing what's necessary, then what's possible, and suddenly you are doing the impossible.
Francis of Assisi

Big things—earning a higher educational degree, mastering a musical instrument, organizing a family holiday event—take big planning. But to accomplish what you want to accomplish, you have to go little step by little step. If you keep looking at what you have yet to do, you'll despair of ever succeeding; but if you take each day as it comes, do what's required, success will be within your grasp before you know it.

15

Relish your relationships.

Give yourself a personal pick-me-up by paging through your mental scrapbook of people and memories, good times and hearty laughs. Bring to mind those who are closest to your heart and give thanks for each of them...for the special things they say and do...for their talents and interests, outlook and unique sense of humor...for all the wonderful ways they have touched your life. Let them know, and you might find that they're giving thanks for you!

16

To cultivate kindness is a valuable part of the business of life.
Samuel Johnson

Authority, power, and prestige command respect. But kindness doesn't command—it naturally receives the respect of others. When you treat people, young and not-so-young, with gentleness, thoughtfulness, generosity, and consideration for their God-given personhood, they willingly respect you. Wherever you go, embrace the best in others by providing an environment that promotes trust, growth, and understanding. Love others, and respect will not be far behind.

17

*Move at the speed of life
instead of the speed of light.*

If you're guilty of taking on too many projects at once, you're not alone! Today you can do things, go places, and learn more than your grandparents would ever have thought possible. But the drawback is this: an overcrowded calendar, a rush from here to there, and an exhausted you at the end of the day. Before you say "yes," make sure you have the time and energy it takes to carry it through.

18

He that respects himself is safe from others.
Henry Wadsworth Longfellow

Being open and honest with others doesn't oblige you to reveal every detail of your life. Kindly but firmly decline to answer probing questions that are not a concern of the person asking. If someone persists in discussing a topic that you'd prefer to keep private, smile sweetly and let his or her words hang in the air. Give yourself the privilege of sharing with those you deem trustworthy; the rest is between you and God.

NOVEMBER

19

*Oh Lord, may I be directed what to do
and what to leave undone.*
Elizabeth Fry

Are your to-dos harassing you? Remind yourself
that you can't do everything—it's impossible!—
but you can do some things. Ask yourself which
things matter the most to you and which things
must get done today. Put the rest on tomorrow's
list...or delegate the tasks to someone else...or decide
that it doesn't matter whether they're done or not,
and choose "not." Free yourself from a tyrannical
to-do list!

20

Times change and we change with them.
Proverb

Family traditions can be heartwarming...or stress-
inducing. If the things you've "always done" over
the holidays have shifted from blessings to burdens
for you or anyone else in the family, it's time to
rethink them. You have changed over the years,
and so has everyone else. Why not get together and
plan a celebration that will be meaningful, doable,
accessible, and affordable for all? You might be
happily surprised how pleasant and relaxed your
holidays become!

NOVEMBER

21

*All emotions are pure which gather you
and lift you up; that emotion is impure
which seizes only one side of your being
and so distorts you.*

Rainer Maria Rilke

Emotions get a bad rap for often being erratic
and irrational. Uncontrolled, emotions are rightly
blamed for outbursts and rash decisions that in
calmer times are sorely regretted. But emotions—
your feelings and passions—can also be the spark
that fires you up to do something your reason says
you can't do or can't be done. It's okay to let your
heart lead you, as long as your head doesn't completely get left behind.

22

A word out of season may mar a whole lifetime.

Proverb

When you're among others, you're entitled to say
what you mean and mean what you say. But if the
conversation gets contentious, uncomfortable, or
mean-spirited, it's time to bow out. Make no effort
to correct or contradict someone who dares you to
do so; ignore those who bring up hot-button issues
just to get people talking. You're not obliged to
approve of what others say or believe to accept who
they are.

NOVEMBER

23

*Misfortune is never mournful to the soul
that accepts it; for such do always see that
in every cloud is an angel's face.*
Jerome

Pay attention to real-life stories about people who
have overcome major obstacles in their lives. Almost
without exception they will tell you that going
through adversity has brought them strength, insight, confidence, and understanding that they never
knew they possessed. Many report that the difficult
experience drew them closer to God and deepened
their faith. It's hard to be grateful for misfortune,
yet there is still reason to give thanks.

24

*You will break the bow if you
keep it always bent.*
Proverb

Thank God for the gift of human resiliency! You
can bounce back from a few sleepless nights, a
couple skimpy or skipped meals, or a string of
long working days. And during the holiday season,
who doesn't stretch to get things done? But if the
occasional time-and-mind stretch becomes your new
normal, your ability to maintain good emotional
and physical health will suffer. No matter how busy
you are, take a break...so you won't.

25

In everything give thanks.
1 Thessalonians 5:18

Counting your blessings sounds so cliché, yet there's nothing trite about the wealth of good gifts you've been given. Start with life itself! Think of the wonders of all creation...the blessing of people you love and who love you...the food you're able to put on the table...the roof over your head...the ability to reach out to God in prayer. (And if nothing you've received moves you to give thanks, at least give thanks for what you've escaped!)

26

With the right tension,
yarn can become a sweater.

Stress puts the push and pull in life. It pushes you to meet a deadline, organize your day, and use time wisely. It pulls you toward helpful tools that will make things easier for you, and to bed after a long day. Like many things, stress is beneficial in moderation, but harmful when it takes over your thinking and decisions, emotions and activities. Listen to what stress is telling you—get moving or take it easy.

27

Enthusiasm gives life to what is invisible.
Madame de Staël

Once you have a vision of what you would like to see happen—during the holidays or any other time— do everything in your power to make it reality. Others may not go along with you right away, but genuine cheerfulness, commitment, and enthusiasm are difficult to resist. Focus on being the example you want them to emulate; show, rather than tell, what kind of atmosphere you want to create. Take responsibility for making it real!

November

28

A friend in need is a friend indeed.

When a friend or family member rearranges their schedule to meet your needs or bends over backward to accommodate you, thank them from the bottom of your heart! Their actions are proof that love always shows itself in meaningful and practical ways. Keep in mind what your willingness to change your plans at a moment's notice for the sake of someone else says about your commitment to the relationship and your love for them.

29

The greater our hurry, the longer the way;
the greater our patience, the sooner we
reach the goal.
        Proverb

It's okay to change your mind. The passage of time gives you a chance to investigate ideas and see if they hold water in real life...personal experience offers practical knowledge that changes the way you look at things...the discernment of others may have enlightened, broadened, or modified your thinking. Let your opinions about social issues, politics, and religion be tested and found true; only then can you live what you believe with well-founded conviction.

30

Have patience with all the things,
but first of all with yourself.
        Francis de Sales

True growth takes time. Your entire life is a process of becoming, of maturing, of learning. Give heartfelt thanks to God as you discern each new bud of growth—an experience that helps you understand more about yourself and the world...the self-confidence it takes to form and maintain healthy and wholesome relationships...the growth that comes as you allow God's Spirit to work freely in your heart. Each bud, in its own time, will blossom beautifully.

God still
works miracles...
every day.

DECEMBER

Many, Lord my God, are the wonders you have done,
the things you planned for us.
Psalm 40:5 NIV

This month, as we celebrate the miracles of Jesus' birth, the star over Bethlehem, and angels' songs breaking through the darkness, it's easy to forget that God continues to work miracles in our lives today.

Consider the miracles of life and breath, the light of thought and imagination, the heavenly ring of faith, hope, and love. Despite all the studied explanations in the world, there is still the wonder of a blossom opening in spring, a rainbow spanning the sky, and the sun's rays skipping over rippling water.

How about the unexpected opportunity that came your way...the special friend that crossed your path "by chance"...the blessings you have reaped without ever having planted...the good place you have come to in life that you never could have planned? In all these things, you are looking at the hand of God; you are experiencing the gift of a miracle.

This month, you're sure to hear, "Remember the reason for the season." When you do, think of the miracle of God-among-us in Jesus, and the miracles that surround you every day.

DECEMBER

1

Hope is faith holding out its hand in the dark.
George Iles

You can be an optimist and a realist at the same time. While you're not afraid to see things as they are—warts and all—there's always hope for the better. Hope tells you that tough times don't last forever (really!) and miracles do happen (really!). Even if circumstances are slow to change, you can change the way you see them. Do all you can to bring the best out of even the most difficult situation.

2

Love grows by service.
Charlotte Perkins Gilman

"I love you" are important words to say, and say often. Yet without loving actions to go with them, the words are simply sentimental pleasantries. Make it a point to give the gift of love not solely with sweet words or ribbon-wrapped gifts, but with gestures that show your love—a visit to a relative who's been asking about you...a phone call to hear the voice of a faraway friend...a favor done before you're even asked.

D ECEMBER

3

Spend an evening with the stars.

Not all stars are dancing on television—the most wondrous ones of all are right above your head every night! Look up and marvel at the miracle of twinkling stars and the brightly shining moon. Let the depth of the skies remind you that the world is full of frontiers yet to be explored, mysteries to be solved, discoveries to be made. And what's true of the universe is true of you, too: embrace the awesome wonder of life!

4

Be still, and know that I am God.
Psalm 46:10

Doing nothing isn't always doing nothing. Sit still in a public place and learn as you observe how people speak and act. Stop and listen to a group of carolers, letting the sound of their voices lift your heart and soul. Stand by a window and watch the snow fall, or go outside and enjoy the feeling of sunshine bathing your face and wind blowing through your hair. Do nothing...and discover the "something" you would otherwise miss.

DECEMBER

5

Goodness that preaches undoes itself.
Ralph Waldo Emerson

What you see with your own eyes carries far more weight than what someone tells you—it's true for you and for others, too. That's why it's far better to let your actions speak for themselves rather than announce the good things you've done and relate stories aimed at highlighting your accomplishments. Similarly, you don't have to rely on what others tell you about miracles, either. Just open the eyes of your heart, see for yourself, and believe!

6

The real voyage of discovery consists not in seeking new landscapes, but in having new eyes.
Marcel Proust

If you were to exercise one arm only, your other arm would become noticeably weaker, perhaps useless. The same is true if you exercise human reasoning only and rarely or never think imaginatively, intuitively, or spiritually. Soon you'd rely exclusively on human reasoning, as it would feel so much more natural and comfortable than spiritual thinking. Yet it's not earthly analysis, but heavenly inspiration, that experiences God's love, His presence, and everyday miracles.

7

*Simplicity is making the journey
of this life with just baggage enough.*
Charles D. Warner

As time passes, you begin to determine what's important in life—possessions or people, things or experiences, status or values, popularity or godliness. As soon as you notice a gap between what you're thinking, saying, doing, or buying and a higher, more spiritual course, pick the higher road. Cast off what you realize is trivial, wasteful, or petty, no matter how long it's been part of your life. Choose to travel light into the days ahead.

8

Eye hath not seen, nor ear heard, neither have entered into the heart of man, the things which God hath prepared for them that love him.
1 Corinthians 2:9

Sometimes, God's plan for you may be clear in your mind; at other times, however, you might wonder if what you're doing has a God-given purpose—and if so, what is it? Wherever you are right now, you can rest assured that God can use your words, talents, and presence to work a miracle in someone's day. Where there are people who need a friendly smile, a helping hand, an encouraging word, there's always a purpose for you.

DECEMBER

9

*When you drink from the stream,
remember the source.*
　　　　Proverb

The many blessings you enjoy today have come
from God through the work and wisdom of others—parents, relatives, teachers, friends, mentors,
ministers, counselors. The holiday season is a good
time to send a card or note of thanks to someone
whose guidance has enriched your life. Remember
the person whose words encouraged you to go on...
whose belief in you gave you a second chance...
whose presence has made a big, big difference.

10

God gives the nuts, but he does not crack them.
　　　　Franz Kafka

How nice if God would instantly drop into our
lap a cash-stuffed purse...a runway-ready body...
a sparkling clean house. What great miracles! But
He doesn't do it that way, does He? There are no
instant solutions to tough problems or quick fixes
for long-neglected responsibilities. The real miracles
lie in your God-given ability to think, act, work,
and accomplish—do your best, and then you can
leave the rest to Him!

DECEMBER

11

*If instead of a gem, or even a flower, we should cast
the gift of a loving thought into the heart of a friend,
that would be giving as the angels give.*
George MacDonald

This Christmas, give those you love something
they can hold in their hearts, instead of their hands.
Relate a story from the past that shows them at
their best...praise them for what they have accomplished this year...tell them how much they mean
to you and why...compliment their strengths and
encourage their highest dreams and ideals. Your
words will sound sweet to their ears, and, we will be
given from the heart valued more than a gift given
from your wallet.

12

No one tests the depth of a river with both feet.
Proverb

Enthusiasm and a can-do attitude are great assets,
but prudence and judgment are necessary partners.
You may envision hosting a five-course dinner, but
a buffet or potluck might better fit your budget. A
showcase holiday home may be your dream, but
this year, perhaps you don't really have time to decorate the entire house. Your reasonable expectations
and realistic considerations go a long way toward
giving whatever you do a greater chance of success.

DECEMBER

13

*How can we send the highest love
to another if we do not have it for ourselves?*
Prentice Mulford

Give everyone around you a gift—love yourself.
It's only through honoring, respecting, and valu-
ing yourself that you're able to extend the same to
others. Self-confidence gives you the power to help,
encourage, and inspire others...it frees you from un-
healthy dependence to wholesome interdependence.
When you take responsibility for your health and
wellbeing, you're releasing someone else to focus on
his or her own health and wellbeing. Self-love and
love for others go together!

14

*Of all the paths a man could strike into,
there is, at any given moment, a best path.*
Thomas Carlyle

Imagine moving through a cafeteria line, tray at
the ready. If you're serious about eating healthy,
there are some dishes you'll pass on and others
you'll take. From all that's available, it's within your
power to prepare a delicious and good-for-you meal.
Similarly, there are many ways to view the holiday
season, from "bah! humbug!" to "deck the halls." If
you want to experience a joyous Christmas, choose
the thoughts and attitude that will make it that way.

DECEMBER

15

*Take rest; a field that has rested
gives a bountiful crop.*
  Ovid

There's always more you can do—more gifts to
buy, more cookies to bake and decorate, more
ornaments to hang on the tree. Yet sleep—so easily
cut short during this busy season—is essential if
you want to do anything well. When you're rested,
you're less susceptible to tension and stress, and you
can actually enjoy the festivities. If some things have
to remain undone, let them go; just don't let go of a
good night's sleep.

16

*There is nothing more beautiful
than cheerfulness in an old face.*
  Jean Paul Richter

Regardless of your age, a smile is your best acces-
sory. Share your smile with the young, because so
many need your encouragement and crave your
approval. Share your smile with the elderly, because
so many wonder if they're still wanted...still loved.
Share your smile with your friends, because there's
no one who's so immune from trouble that a genuine smile isn't appreciated. The more joy and love
you purposefully give to others, the more that smile
will grow.

DECEMBER

17

*God divided the hand into fingers
so that money would slip through.*
Martin Luther

Money slips through fingers, but often in the wrong way—it's spent carelessly, selfishly, or frivolously. Yet the blessing of money, like all God's blessings, is meant to be shared. Even if your finances are stretched right now, give yourself the joy of sharing. A small amount may feed a hungry person...buy a toy for a child...combine with other small amounts to give a homeless family a roof over their heads. Let your money slip the right way!

18

*All the great blessings of my life
are present in my thoughts today.*
Phoebe Cary

Why all the preparations, rushing around, laughter, visiting, gatherings, good feelings, and bright lights? 'Tis the season, without a doubt! Yet most women could use an antidote to feeling overwhelmed, succumbing to stress, or wishing it were all over already. If you can relate, step back for a moment and remember why you're doing what you're doing—it's to nurture family ties, remember cherished friends, and celebrate the gift of God in Jesus.

December

19

*The greatest things in life are the ordinary,
everyday humanities: Speaking kindly to people,
speaking kindly of people, doing kindness for people.*
Fred D. Van Amburgh

Every person you meet and all those around you
(yes, even that hard-to-get-along-with relative!) is
like a priceless piece of pottery: precious in God's
eyes. Yet not every person realizes what they're
worth, and many are carrying burdens of heart and
soul that you may never suspect. Be the woman
God has meant you to be by handling others with
care. Be kind and gentle in thought, word, and
action among friends, family, and strangers alike.

20

*You can make more friends in two months
by becoming interested in other people than
you can in two years by trying to get other
people interested in you.*
Dale Carnegie

When chit-chatting at social gatherings, forget
about yourself. Instead, focus on others. Turn small
talk into a scavenger hunt by moving beyond the
basics to discover their interests and passions, plans
and projects. Avoid questions that can be easily
answered with "yes" or "no" in favor of "why" questions likely to generate longer and more thoughtful
answers. Even if you never meet the person again,
your time will have been well (and pleasingly) spent.

DECEMBER

21

*God gave us memory that we might
have roses in December.*
James M. Barrie

For many, the holiday season brings to mind
happier times—the springtime of love and new
birth...a summer of joy and abundance. Let your
cherished memories of the past remind you that
every winter comes to an end. Just as the seasons
change, the seasons of life change, too. If this
Christmas won't be joyous for you, let it be
blessed with the comfort of God's presence.
Roses will bloom in your life again.

22

*To tend, unfailingly, unflinchingly,
toward a goal is the secret of success.*
Anna Pavlova

Loose ends are like loose shoe laces—if you don't
tie them up, they will trip you up. Get everything
you can in place now, without skipping any necessary details. Wouldn't it be nice to have extra time
on your hands before company comes, rather than
rushing around at the last minute? It's possible!
Take care of the small stuff now so it doesn't turn
into big stuff on the big day.

DECEMBER

23

Let thy words be few in the midst of many.
Teresa of Avila

In most social holiday gatherings, words fly in every direction! Very often, however, some of the words— ill-advised, carelessly chosen, or badly put—do great harm. Even though the one who speaks them may forget they ever escaped her lips, her thoughtless words have the power to hurt feelings and damage relationships. When conversations or discussions heat up, let your silence keep you from wielding unwieldy words.

24

Silent night, holy night!
Traditional Hymn

Today, carve out some time for your heart and soul. Though you may have celebrated numerous holiday seasons, choose to make this one especially meaningful by spending time with God. Take your imagination to Bethlehem's stable and see the Baby Jesus lying in a manger...walk the hills and hear the angels proclaim His birth...look up at the stars and pray for God's light to guide your life, always toward Him. Embrace the miracle of Christmas.

DECEMBER

25

Thanks be to God for his indescribable gift!
2 Corinthians 9:15 NIV

God sent His Son Jesus into the world for a good reason—to open a relationship with you. Certainly no one else possessed, or will possess, the holiness required to enter the presence of God, who is completely holy, good, and perfect. Jesus is the bridge from heaven to earth, bringing God's love and His grace to all—including you. No matter who you are, where you are, or what you have done, He came for you.

26

When love and skill work together, expect a masterpiece.
John Ruskin

Have you ever taken time to discover where your interests and your ability, resources, and opportunities intersect? That's the place you want to be! Right there is where God has opened a door for you, so walk—no, leap!—through it. Don't let fear or hesitation keep you from going forward when you've got a green light, but go with every bit of energy and enthusiasm you have. It's a work of heart that creates a work of art.